HOMICIDE SURVIVORS:

Misunderstood Grievers

By
Judie A. Bucholz, Ph.D.

Death, Value and Meaning Series
Series Editor: John D. Morgan

Baywood Publishing Company, Inc.
AMITYVILLE, NEW YORK

Library of Congress Catalog Number: 2001052913
ISBN: 0-89503-268-6 (cloth)

Library of Congress Cataloging-in-Publication Data

Bucholz, Judie., 1958-
    Homicide survivors : misunderstood grievers / by Judie A. Bucholz.
        p. cm. - - (Death, value, and meaning series)
    Includes bibliographical references and index.
    ISBN 0-89503-268-6
      1. Murder victims' families. 2. Homicide- -Psychological aspects. 3. Bereavement. I. Title. II. Series

HV6515 .B85 2002
362.88- -dc21   2001052913

Table of Contents

Dedication

In loving memory of my husband Daniel Bucholz,
the other homicide victims mentioned in this book:
Lisa, Raymond, Stacey, Tommie, Sharon, Butch, Ronnie, Ben,
Rose's mother, Rita's mother, Laura, Corn, T-Dog, Sherman,
and all homicide survivors left behind to carry on.

Introduction

> Each man must find within himself the various methods to contain
> and control the pain and confusion within. There are no ready-made
> answers. It is a slow process of rediscovery, where denial or flight
> from the inward turmoil is the antithesis of self-healing. We go
> that road alone. We may be helped but we cannot be pushed or
> misdirected. We are our own self-healers [1].

Losing a loved one is an almost unavoidable human experience and
coping with the loss of a loved one is considered one of the most
demanding human endeavors [2]. Sudden death complicates grief and
violent death complicates it even further. Homicide is viewed as an

> adverse stimulus that mobilizes so much painful affect that
> psychological adaptive mechanisms are overwhelmed, initiating
> the alternating responses of hyperactivity and hypoactivity
> [3, p. 217].

Because of the nature of murder and other people's fear of their own
mortality, homicide survivors are often disenfranchised or isolated by
family and society. They are left to heal on their own. Additionally, the
homicide survivor is frequently labeled and victimized by society, which
prolongs the healing process.

No one has provided guidelines on how to grieve a death due to
murder. The survivor must confront the personal and social reality
of the loss, not only the loss of the loved one, but also the loss of dreams,
of hopes, and of a future. While there are some characteristics common
in this type of traumatic bereavement, the homicide survivor must find
his or her own way to deal with

> the blackest hell accompanied by a pain so intense that even breath-
> ing becomes an unendurable labor [4].

This book offers an interpretation of personal accounts of homicide
survivors in order to understand the particular nature of homicide

1

bereavement. This book is written for homicide survivors and those that want to help them.

Thirteen homicide survivors participated in this study. The survivors consisted of four men and nine women between the ages of twenty-four and sixty-seven who have experienced the murder of a family member. Although homicide bereavement is considered traumatic, it is hoped this research will expand the knowledge of this type of bereavement rather than label it as "pathology."

Limitations of the Study

The research discussed was a qualitative study using a phenomenologically inspired perspective to better understand the experience of homicide bereavement. As a qualitative research project, there are limitations inherent in the design. This refers to issues of reliability and validity.

The research study was restricted to a very small population. Thirteen people, identified as homicide survivors, were interviewed. All participants were volunteers. All experienced the murder of a loved one. While I attempted to include a diverse group of participants based on ethnicity, age, gender, marital status, sexual orientation, and socioeconomic status, the findings are applicable to the specific people involved in this study. All but one person in the study was a member of the Parents of Murdered Children (POMC) and Other Homicide Survivors support group. Similar findings may or may not be found in homicide survivors who do not attend support groups. The study does not meet the requirements of generalizability. Transferability, rather than generalizability, is a more appropriate measure for qualitative data. Transferability refers to the transfer of findings where the contexts are similar.

Throughout this book the terms bereavement, grief, and mourning are used. *Bereavement* refers to the state of having suffered a loss. "Bereavement simply means that something you once had is no longer yours" [5, p. 4]. The term *grief* refers to experiencing or responding to the loss. "It is the pain a person feels when someone or something that was important in his or her life is no longer present" [5, p. 5]. *Mourning* refers to the cultural and/or public display of grief through one's behaviors.

> Mourning is how our cultural background (nationality, ethnicity, religion) teaches us how we should respond, and how we think others will expect us to respond to our losses [5, p. 6].

Homicide, as defined by the U.S. Department of Justice, is murder and nonnegligent manslaughter, which is the willful killing of one human being by another [6].

December 24th, 1995 my husband Dan and I were visiting my sister for the Christmas holidays. It was our first Christmas together and we wanted to share it with my family. We were at my sister's house getting ready to drive to Grandma's house for dinner. As Julie, my sister, and I were getting things together, her husband, Jeff received a phone call from the hospital. Jeff was on call at Saint Elizabeth's Hospital where he worked as an Emergency Room Physician. Julie and Jeff were attending to the call while I was packing the food we prepared to take to Grandma's house. Dan went outside to smoke a cigarette and to move the car that I had gotten stuck in the snow earlier that morning. He always said I could not drive properly. We were running late, so things were very chaotic. In the midst of all the fuss, barking dogs, screeching bird, blasting television, etc., I saw red flashing lights in the dining room window. I yelled for my sister and her husband and they went outside to see what was going on. I started to follow them but was stopped by the ringing telephone. I thought it was the hospital calling back so I answered the phone. After I finished the call, I went outside. My sister and her husband where kneeling in the snow in front of my car. My sister immediately told me to go back inside the house. I asked why and she told me just to get back inside the house. Jeff then shouted, "Someone shot Dan!" I saw Dan lying in the snow. I ran over to where he was. There was blood coming from his nose and mouth. I started talking to him, rubbing his face trying to get him to wake up but he just stared straight ahead not moving or talking. He was so cold. Julie and Jeff started CPR; even though there were police, firemen, and an ambulance crew standing around, no one was doing anything. I knew Dan was going to be all right, Jeff was an emergency room physician and Julie was an intensive care nurse. It is their job to save lives. I knew Dan would be fine. It never entered my mind that there was a real problem. After the ambulance crew loaded Dan in the ambulance and the police pushed my car out of the snow bank, Julie and I were permitted to go to the hospital. The receptionist at the hospital told my sister that Dan was not there but of course he was there, it is where the ambulance crew said they were going and Jeff had insisted on that particular hospital because it is a level-two trauma center. After several minutes of checking the computer system, a big male orderly came from the other side of the emergency room and said there was a "John Doe" in the other room but they did not know who he was. They would see if that was my husband. My sister and I were taken out of the hospital waiting room and moved to a private room to wait, probably because of all the blood on Julie's clothes, hands, and face, not to mention the teeth in her pocket from Dan's mouth. After twenty minutes or so, a young female surgical resident came into the room. She showed me Dan's military identification card and asked me if I knew who it was. I told her it was my husband and she then said, "I'm sorry to tell you he expired." "Expired? What does that mean expired? Milk expires, food expires, people don't expire. They don't have a date stamped on their foreheads. What do you mean he expired?" I could not believe nor did I want to believe what she was saying to me. I was hysterical. My sister finally said, "Jude, he's dead." December 24th, 1995 my husband was murdered and my living hell started. To this day, no one knows why, no one has been arrested, and because I am his wife (and 85 percent of the people murdered are killed by someone known to them) I'm considered a "suspect."

My experience as a homicide survivor has given me a unique perspective and experiential base for examining the phenomenon of homicide bereavement. As a homicide survivor, I am able to have contact with a population that generally keeps to itself, a population that does not trust "outsiders." The intent of this book is to help the reader understand the homicide griever's situation, both as one who grieves and one who grieves within a social context, as one who confronts horrific death at the personal level as well as at the social level. My goal is to normalize that which by society's terms is abnormal and to show how some people survive the unsurvivable.

The following pages provide a review of the literature on what is considered normal and abnormal grief. Abnormal grief is generally approached from a psychological perspective often leading to a diagnosis of post traumatic stress disorder. The nature or abnormality of death by murder often leads to societal isolation or disenfranchisement, which further victimizes the homicide survivor. I suspect it is not until the homicide survivor comes to terms with the traumatic event and its consequences, irrespective of society's definition or expectations, that a healing bereavement process can begin. Looking at grief from the homicide survivor's perspective might help depathologize it and help the survivor get back into mainstream society.

Grief is generally studied from one of four perspectives. The basic theoretical perspectives of bereavement can be classified as psychoanalytic, psychoanalytic-cognitive, behavior oriented, and cognitive stress model [7]. I have also included a list of common elements in the latest grief theories.

Psychoanalytic Perspective

The psychoanalytic perspective is based on a clinical diagnosis where certain mental pathologies prevent the bereaved from recovering from the death of a loved one [8, 9]. Freud's concept of loss, outlined in *Mourning and Melancholia* [8] became the cornerstone of psychoanalytic thought on death, depression, and grief. Basically, he believed that grief was a normal reaction to the death of a loved one. Freud believed that the bereaved experiences catharsis by disengaging from the deceased and placing energy into a new relationship. If a person did not disengage, or work through grief, the pathological condition of melancholia (depression) would result and recovery from the death of a loved one would not be possible.

Besides the social taboo regarding death, psychological theories discouraged interest in emotions such as grief [10]. Interest in bereavement grew as the effects of World War II, the results of bereavement research and clinical studies [9, 11], and the theorizing in psychiatry and psychology [12-18] led to the conclusion that the grief process was long and painful with a wide range of somatic and psychological problems.

According to Miles and Demi [19], the focus on grief in the 1970s paralleled the increased interest in death and dying fostered by the writings of Becker [20], Fiefel [21], Glaser and Strauss [22, 23], Kastenbaum and Aisenberg [24], Kübler-Ross [25], Quint [26], Schneidman [27], Weisman [28], and others. The hospice movement, which centered on issues of terminal illness, also served to focus attention on the grief process as it related to terminal illness [29].

Stages of Grief

Stages or phases of grief were popularized by Kübler-Ross [25] (during her work with terminally ill patients) in her book *Death and Dying*. Initially Kübler-Ross identified the stages as consecutive steps but later emphasized that people do not always experience the stages in an orderly or sequential fashion. She saw the stages as overlapping or consecutive. Stages or phases are used to explain the bereavement process in most psychoanalytical theories.

Bowlby [30], Doyle [31], Glick, Weiss, and Parkes [32], Kübler-Ross [25], Pollock [33], and Westberg [34] have identified various stages or phases of grief. Basically the stages are described as follows. Stage 1: attempts to limit the survivor's awareness of the death. This stage includes the initial shock, denial, and isolation felt by the bereaved. Stage 2: consists of the awareness that the loved one is gone. This allows for emotional release such as crying seen at the funeral rites and other family gatherings. Stage 3: begins the sadness or depression typically associated with death. Stage 4: involves acceptance and resolution on the part of the bereaved that the loved one is dead and that life must go on without them.

The stage or phase model of bereavement has been useful in explaining the process of grief as a normal part of the life cycle. Sooner or later everyone experiences the death of someone they love and the stage or phase model provides a framework for understanding the grief process. The stage model has been criticized for being developed from small, non-representative samples, not addressing the individuality of the bereaved, and for not using comparison groups in the studies [31, 35-37]. Overall, there has been a general agreement among the various researchers of the symptomology of grief, but not in the conceptualization of the process of grief. Worden [38, 39], for example, thought the stage or phase theory was acceptable since mourning is considered a process but that the stage model, although a basic explanation of grief, did not describe the process of grief. He developed the tasks of mourning as an explanation of that process.

Tasks of Grief

Worden [38, 39] criticized the stage models of grief as taken too literally. His concern is that those who deviate from the stages are labeled as dysfunctional or sick, when in fact the bereaved are very adaptive to the death. Worden developed the "tasks of mourning" which he insists empowers the bereaved to take an active role in their recovery rather than go through the passive stages of grief. Worden felt the tasks were

> more consonant with Freud's concept of grief work and imply that the mourner needs to take action and can do something. . . . In other words, the mourner sees the concept of phases as something to be passed through, while the tasks approach gives the mourner some sense of leverage and hope that there is something that he or she can actively do [39, p. 35].

Worden believed that the tasks of mourning were necessary activities to get the griever through the bereavement process. Not completing the tasks would cause the bereaved to become "stuck" in grief, which would lead to pathology. The tasks consist of accepting the reality of the loss, working through the pain of grief, adjusting to an environment in which the deceased is missing, and emotionally relocating the deceased and moving on with life. Worden describes emotionally relocating the deceased as finding

> an appropriate place for the dead in their [survivor's] emotional lives—a place that will enable them to go on living effectively in the world [39, p. 17].

Worden refers to Schuchter and Zisook:

> A survivor's readiness to enter new relationships depends not on "giving up" the dead spouse but on finding a suitable place for the spouse in the psychological life of the bereaved—a place that is important but that leaves room for others [40, p. 117].

Psychoanalytic-Cognitive Perspective

The psychoanalytic-cognitive perspective is based on the notions of bonding and attachment where grief is conceived as separation anxiety [11, 41, 42]. Bowlby [41] contended that attachment is an expression of affective needs within humans, as well as animals. Attachments come from a need for security and for safety. Much of Bowlby's earlier work was describing and explaining normal and so-called pathological reactions when attachments are severed. According to Bowlby, grief is a subjective experience from the loss of a love object and is considered a normal reaction. He explains the experiences, symptoms, behaviors, pain, and purpose of grief and mourning in human beings and then makes an analogy to other primates. "The mourning responses of animals show what primitive biological processes are at work in human beings" [38, p. 9]. It is the similarity of separation responses that convinces Bowlby that grief responses are instinctual, adaptational, and valuable for survival. Death is viewed as an unwanted separation from an attachment figure and childhood experiences in bonding affect the outcome of bereavement. According to Bowlby [43] mourning in mentally healthy adults lasted longer than previously suggested and that responses that were considered pathological were in fact common and normal. These responses include anger directed at third parties, the self, and the lost person; disbelief that the loss occurred; and a tendency to search, often unconsciously, for the lost person in hope of reunion. The psychoanalytic-cognitive perspective is different from the psychoanalytic view in that a relationship with the deceased is continued and that the continued relationship with the deceased provides comfort to the bereaved. Grief is resolved when new relationships are developed and new structures of meaning have been established.

Behavior Oriented Perspective

The behavior perspective [44, 45] conceptualizes grief as causing psychological and physiological changes in the mourner. These changes are considered greatly influenced by environmental factors. Parkes describes grief as

> a complex time-consuming process in which a person gradually changes his (her) view of the world and the places and habits by means of which he (she) orients and relates to it [11, p. 465].

Grief involves making psychologically real an external event that is not desirable and for which coping patterns do not exist [46]. Averill [12] hypothesized that bereavement has significance beyond the well being of the individual. He suggested bereavement fulfills an evolutionary societal need—the maintenance of the long-term social bonds needed for survival of the species. This perspective's emphasis is on external factors such as social supports.

Attig [47] suggests that grieving is a process of relearning the world in which we live. Instead of mastering the idea that one's life is different because a loved one has died, Attig says we relearn our world. Relearning involves investment of ourselves "as whole persons, in all facets of our life all at once" [47, p. 13]. Through the relearning the survivor reestablishes self-confidence, self-esteem, and an identity.

> We strive to adapt our behaviors and daily life patterns to new circumstances not of our own choosing and to recover our own sense of daily purpose [47, p. 14].

Cognitive Stress Perspective

The cognitive stress model insists that the stress of death exceeds the limits of the bereaved's coping ability and that grief is a process of coping, learning, and adapting to the stress [48, 49].

Demi [50, 51] proposed a model of bereavement that synthesizes grief, life transitions, stress, and coping theories. Demi suggests that the bereaved experience at least three crisis periods during bereavement and the outcome of each crisis is a potential turning point in the survivor's life. The outcome may lead to improved health and greater maturity or to poorer health and psychosocial deterioration.

Horowitz [52] considers the response to death to be a general stress response syndrome. According to Horowitz, a stressful event contains news that is severely out of line with the way an individual believes himself or herself to be in the world. This causes a sudden and powerful breach in the individual's security and violates his or her assumptive world. Following a serious life event and immediate efforts at coping, the individual typically undergoes the following responses: outcry, denial and numbing, intrusion, working through, and completion. Outcry involves fear, sadness, and rage. Denial and numbing involves the refusal to face the memory of the trauma. Intrusion includes the unbidden thoughts and images, feelings, behaviors, and physiological responses associated with the event. Working through the stress involves facing the reality of what happened, addressing meanings, mourning, and developing new plans. Completion is the integration of thoughts, feelings, and memories that end the intrusions. Stress models of grief consider bereavement a stressful life event and offer an explanation for the physical health consequences of bereavement. Pathological responses include being overwhelmed, dazed, confused, and swept away by immediate emotional reactions; panic or exhaustion, dissociative reactions, and reactive psychosis; maladaptive avoidances such as resorting to extreme measures to deny pain; flooded and impulsive states; psychological disruptions, anxiety and depressive reactions; and character distortions such as long term inability to work, create, or feel emotions.

Basically, bereavement begins with shock, followed by adjustment, and resolved with the development of new life patterns. Specific somatic symptoms are identified for each stage or phase of bereavement. A time frame for grief is determined as normal for each stage and a deviation from that is diagnosed as complicated, abnormal, delayed or distorted.

Newer Models of Mourning

Neimeyer [53] identifies the following elements as common to a "new wave" of grief theories:

(a) skepticism about the universality of a predictable "emotional trajectory" that leads from psychological disequilibrium to readjustment, coupled with an appreciation of more complex patterns of adaptation,

(b) a shift away from the presumption that successful grieving requires "letting go" of the one who has died, and toward a recognition of the potential healthy role of maintaining continued symbolic bonds with the deceased,

(c) attention to broadly cognitive processes entailed in mourning, supplementing the traditional focus on the emotional consequences of loss,

(d) greater awareness of the implications of major loss for the bereaved individual's sense of identity, often necessitating deep-going revisions in his or her self-definition,

(e) increased appreciation of the possibility of life-enhancing "post traumatic growth" as one integrates the lessons of loss, and

(f) broadening the focus of attention to include not only the experience of individual grievers, but also the reciprocal impact of loss on families and broader (sub) cultural groups [53, pp. 109-110].

Researchers have tried to describe the process of grief and have also tried to establish parameters of normalcy of grief. It is helpful to review this to show how a person becomes pathologized. Most early researchers of grief, particularly grief involving traumatic circumstances, have looked at bereavement as a clinical disorder. The next section defines abnormal grief and traumatic loss leading to post traumatic stress disorder.

"Abnormal" or Complicated Grief

"Abnormal" grief reactions have been labeled atypical [46], morbid [9], chronic [41, 46], complicated [16, 54], and pathological [55, 56]. These reactions involve absent, delayed, intensified, inhibited, or prolonged aspects of "uncomplicated" or normal bereavement.

Complicated Mourning

Rando [54] identified seven complicated mourning syndromes. They include three syndromes with problems in expression (i.e., absent, delayed, and inhibited grief), three syndromes with skewed aspects (i.e., distorted, conflicted, and unanticipated grief), and one syndrome with a problem with closure (i.e., chronic grief).

Absent grief, also called repressed or masked grief, is distinguished by a void of emotions [57-59]. Absent grief shows up as physical symptoms often similar to those experienced by the deceased prior to death or as a maladaptive behavior such as acting out [60].

Delayed grief is also called inhibited, suppressed, or postponed grief. A survivor may have had an emotional reaction at the time of the loss but the reaction is not considered sufficient for the loss. The reaction is released later and is considered excessive at that time and could lead to somatic complaints [9, 33, 39, 41, 56, 57, 61, 62]. Zisook and his colleagues use a similar term of unresolved grief [63].

Distorted or exaggerated grief is an intense grief reaction in which the survivor feels overwhelmed. Distorted grief is excessive and disabling because the survivor experiences excessive depression and excessive anxiety [9, 39, 59, 64].

Chronic grief is characterized as: excessive in duration without a satisfactory conclusion [39, 65, 66]; yearning for an idealized relationship that never existed [57]; an overly dependent relationship with the deceased [41, 62]; and grief that is continually unremitting [46, 64]. Years later, however, many pathological explanations of bereavement were explained as "normal" reactions [67]. For example, Bonanno et al. [68, 69] found that individuals who fail to "work through" the emotional significance of a loss do not suffer delayed grief or enduring or delayed health difficulties as traditionally assumed.

Recently, "complicated mourning" has replaced the phrase "pathological grief" as a description in which "there is some compromise, distortion, or failure" [54, p. 149].

Even among the mentioned perspectives there is disagreement as to what constitutes "abnormal" bereavement and what is considered normal given the circumstances associated with the death and the survivor's ability to cope with such a traumatic loss. Some researchers look at grief from the psychological perspective as a reaction to a traumatic loss.

Traumatic Loss

Until recently, traumatic death has been approached as either exclusively as a trauma or solely as a loss. Those specializing in bereavement overlooked the trauma brought on by the circumstances of a death, and the trauma experts failed to recognize the loss issues. Rando contends,

> In fact, it's not too much of a stretch, if any, to state that in general traumatologists know little to nothing about loss and, conversely, thanatologists know about the same amount regarding trauma [quoted in 70, p. xv].

Rando goes on to say that thanatologists overutilized the models and treatment expectations of bereavement and that the models and expectations

> . . . may be quite inappropriate for a traumatic death, hurting, rather than merely not helping, the bereaved survivors [quoted in 70, p. xvi].

And that the thanatologists' focus on "loss" misses "the post traumatic sequelae that eventuate when the death involves traumatic characteristics" [quoted in 70, p. xvi].

Traumatic loss includes: 1) deaths that occur suddenly or without warning; 2) deaths that are untimely, including the death of one's child at any age (parents do not expect to outlive their children); 3) deaths involving violence, mutilation, or destruction; 4) situations involving multiple deaths; 5) deaths viewed as random; 6) deaths perceived as "unnecessary" or preventable; and 7) deaths that involve a direct threat to the personal safety of the survivor. In most cases, traumatic loss involves one or more of these factors [54, 71].

Although there are numerous studies dealing with bereavement, only a handful have addressed the unique problems encountered by those who have endured the sudden, traumatic death of a loved one [36, 72, 73].

Rinear [74] lists the most common reactions to the traumatic loss of a loved one as: 1) feelings of shock or numbness; 2) preoccupation with the loss of the deceased; 3) concern with the brutality or suffering associated with the crime; 4) anger toward the suspect(s) or criminal justice system; 5) intense need to know the details of the death; 6) appetite disturbance; 7) disturbance of sleep patterns; 8) feelings of depression and hopelessness so intense there is a feeling of unreality; and 9) inability to put death out of one's mind. These reactions can last several years following the death [75, 76]. Van der Kolk says trauma occurs "when one loses the sense of having a safe place to retreat to within or outside oneself to deal with frightening emotions or experiences" [77, p. 32].

Generally there are affective, cognitive, behavioral, and physiological responses associated with traumatic deaths such as murder [54, 73, 75]. Affective responses include rage, terror, numbness, and feelings of devastation and irritability [4, 78]. Cognitive responses include confusion, memory impairment, and inability to concentrate. Behavioral responses refer to anxiety about the safety of the family and one's self, phobic avoidance of trauma-related stimuli, and social isolation [79]. Physiological responses include appetite and sleep disturbances [8, 81], gastrointestinal, cardiovascular, and immune system changes [82], and increased startle responses [82, 83].

Sudden traumatic death forces the bereaved to question the basic assumptions they previously took for granted [30, 84-88]. These assumptions include that the world is predictable and controllable, that the world is meaningful and operates according to the principles of fairness and justice, that one is safe and secure, that the world is benevolent, and that, generally speaking, other people can be trusted. These assumptions are shattered when a loved one is murdered [89].

Recently there has been a movement for the development of a diagnostic criterion for "traumatic grief" [90, 91]:

The term Traumatic Grief was chosen as it (a) describes more precisely the disorder encompassed by the consensus criteria, (b) is less vague than other terms such as complicated grief or unresolved grief, and (c) is less negative in terms such as morbid or pathologic grief [90].

Traumatic grief is a descendent of the concept of pathological grief, with associations to attachment behavior, separation distress, and traumatic distress. The proposed criteria for traumatic grief includes:

Criterion A
1. The person has experienced the death of a significant other.
2. The response involves intrusive, distressing preoccupation with the deceased person (c.g., yearning, longing, or searching).

Criterion B
In response to the death, the following symptom(s) is/are marked and persistent:
1. Frequent efforts to avoid reminders of the deceased (e.g., thoughts, feelings, activities, people, places);
2. Purposelessness or feelings of futility about the future;
3. Subjective sense of numbness, detachment, or absence of emotional responsiveness;
4. Feeling stunned, dazed, or shocked;
5. Difficulty acknowledging the death (disbelief);
6. Feeling that life is empty or meaningless;
7. Difficulty imagining a fulfilling life without the deceased;
8. Feeling that part of oneself has died;
9. Shattered worldview (e.g., lost sense of security, trust, or control);
10. Assumes symptoms or harmful behaviors of, or related to, the deceased person; and/or
11. Excessive irritability, bitterness, or anger related to the death.

Criterion C
The duration of the disturbance (symptoms listed) is at least two months.

Criterion D
The disturbance causes clinically significant impairment in social, occupational, or other important areas of functioning [90, p. 189].

Grief has also been examined as a different phenomenon with the different types of death. For the purpose of this book, I have limited the review to death by homicide.

Homicide Bereavement

"The symptomatology and management of acute grief" published in the *American Journal of Psychiatry* [9] is regarded as a classic in the field of bereavement. Lindemann worked with family members whose loved ones were killed in Boston's Coconut Grove fire where nearly 500 people lost their lives. His findings were based upon sudden unexpected death of a loved one and are considered fundamental in the field of post traumatic stress. In his work, Lindemann defined the "bereavement syndrome" as a pathological grief reaction characterized by: 1) somatic disturbances; 2) preoccupation with the image of the deceased; 3) guilt resulting from the deceased or circumstances of the death; 4) hostile reactions; and 5) an inability to function as before the death. Lindemann suggested pathological grief occurs as a result of avoiding intense distress experience(s).

Many homicide survivors have adopted the popular stage model of dying as a means of trying to understand their emotions following the death of a loved one. Kübler-Ross' stages of dying are: 1) denial and isolation; 2) anger; 3) bargaining; 4) depression; and 5) acceptance [25]. Sprang, McNeil, and Wright [81] identified five stages, similar to the stages identified by Kübler-Ross [25], of grieving for homicide survivors: 1) shock, denial, and isolation; 2) emotional release; 3) guilt, anger, and resentment; 4) depression; and 5) acceptance, resolution, and adaptation. The bereavement process is dependent upon many factors such as personality, previous experiences with death, and mental health history.

Clinicians working with homicide survivors have noted disproportionate numbers of complicated grief reactions such as anxiety attacks, suicide ideation, and overwhelming rage triggered by trivialities [92]. Noted behavioral changes include phobic avoidance of homicide-related stimuli and increased self-protective measures [36, 93]. In his 1993 study, Parkes states that homicide bereavement is

> particularly conducive to psychopathology. The combination of sudden, unexpected, horrific, and untimely death, with all the rage and guilt which followed and, often, the overwhelming of the family as a support system to the bereaved, are bound to interfere with normal grieving [94, p. 52].

Parkes goes on to say that homicide bereavement interferes with normal grieving by: 1) inducing post traumatic stress—a kind of emotional shock that generates anxiety, depressive avoidance, and vivid mental imagery; 2) evoking intense rage toward the offender and all associated with him or her at a time when there may not be an opportunity to vent that rage effectively; 3) undermining trust in others, including the family, the police, the legal system, and God; and 4) evoking guilt at having survived and at failing to protect the deceased.

> Although grief is a common human experience, mourning for families of murder victims is more profound, more lingering, and more complex than normal grief [3, p. 159].

Homicide presents at least three peculiarities that differentiate it from natural dying: 1) the death is violent—a forceful, suddenly traumatic act; 2) the death is a volition—an intentional act; and 3) the death is a violation—a transgressive act. Rynearson [95] suggests that violence, violation, and volition are associated with syndromal effects. The responses include: 1) post traumatic stress disorder (experiences of intrusive reenactment and avoidance); 2) victimization (rage and a sense of defilement); and 3) compulsive inquiry (a social and psychological need for investigation and punishment of the killer). In the case of homicide, compulsive inquiry may last long after the crime has been solved and the perpetrator punished.

> Homicide bereavement has presented a psychological challenge that cannot be avoided . . . homicide will have a lasting impact on his or her [the survivor's] life, and there is no therapy that is going to offer complete relief [95, p. 343].

Because people do not understand the loss reactions of the homicide survivor, many professionals make a premature diagnosis of complicated mourning. Spungen asks, "The unique quality of grief makes homicide bereavement different, but does it necessarily make the mourning complicated?" [4, p. 31]. Controversy exists in the literature as to what is considered "complicated" mourning for homicide survivors. Even in the symptomatology, there is considerable overlap with operationally defined syndromes such as depression, anxiety, and post traumatic stress disorder [96-98].

After a homicide, the death, police, criminal justice system, and media may overwhelm the survivor. The survivor may experience a variety of responses, which have frequently been labeled post traumatic stress disorder because currently there exists no diagnostic category for complicated bereavement. The responses could be affective, cognitive, behavioral, or psychological. Researchers looking at grief from a psychological perspective often address the traumatic reaction to loss as post traumatic stress disorder.

Post Traumatic Stress Disorder

Studies focused specifically on homicide survivors have found symptoms conforming to post traumatic stress disorder (PTSD) presented in the American Psychiatric Association's *Diagnostic and Statistical Manual of Mental Disorders,* 4th ed. (DSM–IV). PTSD is an anxiety disorder that is precipitated by a stressful life event that would evoke distress in most people and is outside the range of normal human experience such as war, natural disasters, and violent crime (Criterion A). Three clusters capture the symptomatology. The first cluster (Criterion B) consists of cognitive or re-experiencing symptoms, such as having flashbacks, intrusive thoughts, and nightmares. The second cluster (Criterion C) consists of affective symptoms, such as feeling estranged from others, numbing of feelings, and avoidance of activities or reminders of the death. The third cluster (Criterion D) consists of physiological symptoms, such as hyperviligance, irritability, and trouble falling and staying asleep [80, 99]. Symptoms are diagnosed as a disorder if they persist over a period of one month.

Post traumatic stress disorder and associated symptoms (or pathology) are reported in those working with homicide survivors [94, 100-105].

Although there have been studies of homicide survivors, most address the symptomology and pathology and do not address the bereavement process. The purpose of my research was to obtain a description of how homicide survivors define and process their experience of homicide bereavement. It is hoped the information gained from this research will help homicide survivors and their families understand the experience and the pain of murder in a constructive and helpful way.

> The loss of a significant other, in whatever role, is painful. But only when we recognize and understand the reality and unique nature of the pain can we begin to help ease it [106, p. 75].

Most of the literature on bereavement describes grief as normal or abnormal or complicated. Homicide survivors are typically labeled as abnormal or different in their bereavement process. Since homicide is not one of the leading causes of death, those who grieve it can be seen as "abnormal." However, this does not mean that the grief process that follows is "abnormal" or that the survivors of homicide are "abnormal." The treatment or label of abnormality or differentness for homicide survivors may lead to complications in mourning, disenfranchisement, and victimization.

This book was written as an attempt to give voice to homicide survivors. It started as a search for answers to questions I had about why I felt and was treated so differently as a homicide survivor. My quest for answers became the research for a dissertation. My first attempts at getting research on homicide bereavement approved by the dissertation committee met with much resistance. Some committee members felt the subject was taboo or too sensitive a topic for study or that the topic was too close and too personal for me to study since my husband was murdered a year earlier. Some committee members did not want to deal with the reality of murder. In fact it was not until the day of the oral review, nearly one year after the research, that one dissertation committee member finally came to understand that homicide bereavement is often different than other types of bereavement.

My dear friend Dr. Sarah Brabant encouraged me to write this book. She felt my research needed to be shared so that homicide survivors might be better understood and normalized rather than labeled mentally ill or troubled people. I met Sarah at a Sociological Association meeting. A person at the meeting was concerned that I was not "over" my husband's death yet, so he insisted I meet and talk with Sarah about "my problem." Sarah explained to me that sometimes other people's difficulty accepting the reality of murder and the pain it can cause leads them to believe a person is abnormal or sick because the bereaved express their feelings rather than hide them. I was clearly saddened by my husband's death and I often cried just thinking about him. Sarah was the first person I talked to that understood the pain of murder and the pain of being a homicide survivor.

This book is about families that have faced murder and how they have dealt with the trauma. The names have been changed and some of the experiences have been combined in order to show the variety of reactions and ways of coping. In a sense, these stories are constructed; however, they are about real people and real events, they are not fiction. Whenever possible, I have used the survivor's own words. This book is written in a way that will allow the reader to gain a sense of what it is like to be a homicide survivor. It is hoped the information in this book will be used to help homicide survivors and those wanting to comfort them.

The next section contains an introduction of the results of my research on homicide bereavement. I present it here as a guide for the rest of the book. Figure 1 is a visual representation of what is to come. "Stick people" are used so that we do not forget the individualism, the humanness of bereavement. The stick people are joined to remind us that support from others helps homicide survivors, and others who mourn the loss of their loved ones, survive the unsurvivable. Further explanations are found in Parts Two and Three.

Homicide bereavement affects the survivor on a personal and social level. On a personal level, the homicide survivor experiences loss, trauma, and victimization. Personal loss refers to the loss or death of the loved one, the loss of the basic assumptions in life, the loss of

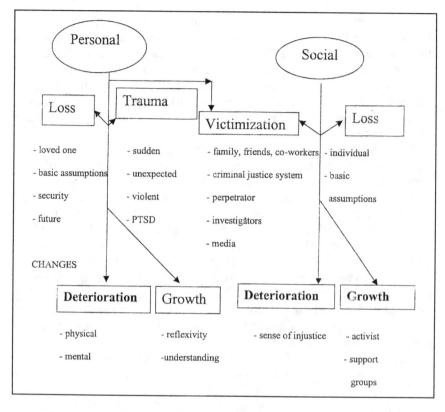

Figure 1. Homicide bereavement chart.

security, and a loss of a future. For the homicide survivor, the loss of basic assumptions in life has to do with facing the harsh reality that the world is not safe and secure, the world is not fair and just, and generally speaking people cannot be trusted. The homicide survivor abruptly learns that bad things do happen to good people, a good "Christian" life does not prevent murder, and that the world is not predictable or controllable. A homicide survivor's personal security is violated when his or her loved one is murdered. The world is no longer considered safe and a preoccupation with the remaining loved ones' security and the homicide survivor's personal security becomes a primary concern. The murder creates an increased sense of vulnerability and this often results in an increase in protective measures such as locks, alarms, and personal protective measures such as traveling in pairs or the purchase of handguns. The loss of a future refers to the life that could have been—the daughter-in-law that will never happen, grandchildren and great grandchildren that will not come, and a sister-in-law that is no longer possible. These personal losses invoke trauma for the homicide survivor.

Personal trauma results from the sudden unexpected death of a loved one. Homicide occurs without warning, there is no time for preparation. Homicide involves the intentional, deliberate act of another person. It is a violent and senseless act that often involves no remorse from the perpetrator. Trauma induces affective, cognitive, and physiological symptoms for the homicide survivor including nightmares, numbing of feelings, intrusive thoughts, and sleep and appetite disturbances. A lack of understanding of the trauma and resultant victimization further traumatizes the homicide survivor.

Society attaches a stigma to murder, leaving the homicide survivor victimized. Family, friends, co-workers, the criminal justice system, perpetrator, media, investigators, and the religious community victimize the homicide survivor on a personal and social level. Family, friends, and co-workers victimize the homicide survivor by their insensitive comments and unrealistic expectations of "recovery." Society perpetuates an expectation of returning to normal or to the way things were after a short period of mourning. This expectation is written in grief literature, self-help books, and advocated by some grief counselors and therapists. The criminal justice system victimizes the homicide survivor repeatedly with each pretrial, trial, sentencing, motions, and appeal hearings. If more than one perpetrator is involved, the series of trials, hearings, and appeals is repeated for each perpetrator. Even with the right to a speedy trial, it is not unusual for a murder case to take two years to get to trial. The perpetrator victimizes the homicide survivor first by taking the loved one's life then by the repeated contact with the homicide survivor through the criminal justice system. Even after the trial, the homicide survivor is victimized each time the perpetrator files for an appeal, leniency, clemency, and/or comes up for parole. If the perpetrator(s) is released from prison, the homicide survivor, and his or her family, become victimized again because of the uncertainty of the perpetrator, by not knowing if the perpetrator will seek revenge toward the homicide survivor or his or her family members. The media also victimizes the homicide survivor. Murders, particularly murders involving children, are generally sensationalized, often at the expense of the homicide survivor. Often without warning, articles are printed on the front page of the newspaper or announced on the television explaining in graphic detail the brutality of the murder. Movies made without the consent of the homicide survivors often change the circumstances surrounding the murder. In many instances the movie places blame on the victim or his or her family. The homicide survivors are helpless to set the record straight or clear their loved one's name and reputation. Strangers actually make money from the murder of the homicide survivor's loved one. The religious community victimizes the homicide survivor by insisting on forgiveness. By forgiving the perpetrator, the religious community and many grief counselor and therapists believe the homicide survivor can "recover" or return to "normal" after his or her loved one has been murdered.

Besides the obvious personal loss, society also suffers a loss as a result of homicide. Society loses an individual, a taxpayer, and contributor to mankind. Society also suffers a loss of some basic assumptions about life. First, that homicide demonstrates that the world is not safe, controlled, or predictable as previously assumed. Second, that killers exist and are likely to strike any one, any time, and anywhere.

As Figure 1 indicates, homicide bereavement results in change on a personal and social level. Change can result in deterioration and/or growth. On a personal level, deteriorating change refers to the mental and physical changes after a murder. The constant high levels of stress and post traumatic stress deteriorate the survivor's physical and mental functioning abilities. Growth refers to the survivor's ability to find meaning in the murder. Through reflexivity, a process of coming to terms with the situation in spite of others and the societal expectations, a survivor can find personal meaning in the murder. The personal meaning can lead to a sense of a higher cause or a deeper understanding in the meaning of life. On a social level, homicide can result in deterioration or growth. Social deterioration refers to the sense of injustice often seen at a murder trial. Lenient punishments, legal technicalities, and plea bargains sometime portray the perpetrator as getting away with murder. This is most obvious in the juvenile justice system when the murderer can be released at the age of 21. Social growth refers to the homicide survivors who become activists seeking legislative changes in the judicial system. The homicide survivor turned activist increases the public's knowledge of the current criminal justice system and seeks change. Social growth also refers to the increase in homicide support groups and support networks. Homicide survivors are often misunderstood grievers. They are generally only understood by other homicide survivors because they are the only ones who have experienced the horrific trauma, stigma, and victimization of murder first hand.

Part One of this book contains ten stories from actual homicide survivors. Part Two contains common reactions of grieving loved ones. The reactions are listed as themes that run throughout the survivor's descriptions of their experience. Part Three contains an analysis of Parts One and Two and some suggestions for helping homicide survivors during their grief journey. At the end of each chapter I have included notes further explaining key points in the chapter as well as references to those notes where applicable.

References

1. B. Eagerman, *The Globe,* p. 10, April 19, 1991.
2. T. H. Holmes and R. H. Rahe, The Social Readjustment Rating Scale, *Journal of Psychosomatic Research, 11,* pp. 213-218, 1967.
3. E. K. Rynearson, The Homicide of a Child, in *Post-Traumatic Therapy and Victims of Violence,* F. Ochberg (ed.), Brunner/Mazel, New York, pp. 213-224, 1998.
4. D. Spungen, *Homicide: The Hidden Victims,* Sage, Thousand Oaks, California, 1998.
5. S. Brabant, *Mending the Torn Fabric: For Those Who Grieve and Those Who Want to Help Them,* Baywood, Amityville, New York, 1996.
6. Bureau of Justice Statistics, *Reports to the Nation on Crime and Justice,* U.S. Department of Justice, Washington, D.C., 1999.
7. M. Cleiren, *Bereavement and Adaptation,* Hemisphere, Washington, D.C., 1993.
8. S. Freud, *Mourning and Melancholia* (Vol. 4), Basic Books, New York, 1917.
9. E. Lindemann, Symptomatology and Management of Acute Grief, *American Journal of Psychiatry, 101,* pp. 141-148, 1944.
10. J. R. Averill, The Functions of Grief, in *Emotions and Personality and Psychopathology,* C. E. Izard (ed.), Plenum Press, New York, pp. 339-367, 1979.
11. C. M. Parkes, The First Year of Bereavement, *Psychiatry, 33,* pp. 444-476, 1970.
12. J. R. Averill, Grief: Its Nature and Significance, *Psychology Bulletin, 70,* pp. 721-748, 1968.
13. J. R. Bowlby, Grief and Mourning in Infancy and Early Childhood, *Psychoanalytic Study of the Child, 15,* pp. 9-52, 1960.
14. J. R. Bowlby, Processes of Mourning, *International Journal of Psychoanalysis, 42,* pp. 317-340, 1961.
15. G. Caplan, *Principles of Preventive Psychiatry,* Basic Books, New York, 1964.
16. G. L. Engel, Is Grief a Disease? A Challenge for Medical Research, *Psychosomatic Medicine, 23,* pp. 18-22, 1961.
17. G. Engel, Psychoanalytic Theory of Somatic Disorder, *Journal of the American Psychoanalytic Association, 15,* pp. 344-365, 1967.
18. G. Groer, *Death, Grief, and Mourning,* Anchor Books, New York, 1967.
19. M. S. Miles and A. S. Demi, Historical and Contemporary Theories of Grief, in *Dying, Death, and Bereavement Theoretical Perspectives and Other Ways of Knowing,* I. B. Corless, B. B. Germino, and M. Pittman (eds.), Jones and Bartlett, Boston, Massachusetts, 1994.
20. E. Becker, *The Denial of Death,* Free Press, New York, 1973.

21. G. L. Feifel, *The Meaning of Death*, McGraw-Hill, New York, 1964.
22. B. Glaser and A. Strauss, *Awareness of Dying*, Aldine, Chicago, 1966.
23. B. Glaser and A. Strauss, *A Time for Dying*, Aldine, Chicago, 1967.
24. R. Kastenbaum and R. B. Aisenberg, *The Psychology of Death*, Springer, New York, 1972.
25. E. Kübler-Ross, *On Death and Dying*, Macmillan, New York, 1969.
26. J. Quint, *The Nurse and the Dying Patient*, Macmillan, New York, 1969.
27. E. Schneidman, *The Deaths of Man*, Quadrangle/The New York Times Book Co., New York, 1973.
28. A. D. Weisman, *Death and Denial*, Behavioral Publications, New York, 1972.
29. S. Stoddard, *The Hospice Movement: A Better Way of Caring for the Dying*, Random House, New York, 1978.
30. J. Bowlby, *Attachment and Loss: Attachment* (Vol. 1), Basic Books, New York, 1969.
31. P. Doyle, *Grief Counseling and Sudden Death*, Charles C. Thomas, Springfield, Illinois, 1980.
32. R. Glick, R. Weiss, and C. M. Parkes, *The First Year of Bereavement*, John Wiley and Sons, New York, 1974.
33. G. H. Pollock, The Mourning—Liberation Process in Health and Disease, *Psychiatric Clinics of North America, 10*, pp. 345-354, 1987.
34. G. E. Westberg, *Good Grief*, Fortress Press, Philadelphia, Pennsylvania, 1971.
35. N. J. Bowman, *Differential Reactions to Dissimilar Types of Death: Specifically the Homicide/Murder*, unpublished doctoral dissertation, International University, San Diego, California, 1980.
36. A. W. Burgess, Family Reaction to Homicide, *American Journal of Orthopsychiatry, 45*, pp. 391-398, 1975.
37. A. F. Poussaint, *The Grief Response Following Homicide*, paper presented at the American Psychological Association, Toronto, Canada, 1984.
38. J. W. Worden, *Grief Counseling and Grief Therapy: A Handbook for the Mental Health Practitioner*, Springer, New York, 1982.
39. J. W. Worden, Grieving a Loss from AIDS, *The Hospice Journal, 7*, pp. 143-150, 1991.
40. S. R. Schuchter and S. Zisook, Treatment of Spousal Bereavement: A Multidimensional Approach, *Psychiatric Annals, 16*, pp. 295-305, 1986.
41. J. Bowlby, *Attachment and Loss—Loss: Sadness and Depression* (Vol. 3), Basic Books, New York, 1980.
42. P. Marris, *Loss and Change*, Routledge and Kegan Paul, London, 1974.
43. J. Bowlby, Attachment and Loss: Retrospective and Prospective, *American Journal of Orthopsychiatry, 52*, pp. 664-678, 1982.
44. J. Gauthier and W. L. Marshall, Grief: A Cognitive-Behavioral Analysis, *Cognitive Therapy Research, 1*, pp. 34-44, 1977.
45. R. Ramsay, Bereavement: A Behavioral Treatment of Pathological Grief, in *Trends in Behavior Therapy*, P. Soden, S. Bates, and W. Dockins (eds.), Academic, New York, 1979.

46. C. M. Parkes, *Bereavement and Studies of Grief in Adult Life*, International Universities Press, Madison, Connecticut, 1972.
47. T. Attig, *How We Grieve Relearning the World*, Oxford University Press, New York, 1996.
48. M. J. Horowitz, N. Wilner, N. Kaltreider, and W. Alvarez, Signs and Symptoms of Posttraumatic Stress Disorder, *Archives of General Psychiatry, 37*, pp. 85-92, 1980.
49. R. S. Lazarus, The Psychology of Stress and Coping, *Mental Health Nursing, 7*, pp. 1-4, 399-418, 1985.
50. A. S. Demi, Hospice Bereavement Programs: Trends and Issues, in *Hospice: The Nursing Perspective*, S. Scraff (ed.), National League of Nursing, New York, pp. 131-151, 1987.
51. A. S. Demi, Death of a Spouse, in *Midlife Loss: Coping Strategies*, R. Kalish (ed.), Sage, Newbury Park, California, pp. 218-224, 1989.
52. M. Horowitz, *Stress Response Syndromes: PTSD, Grief, and Adjustment Disorders* (3rd Edition), Jason Aronson, Northvale, New Jersey, 1997.
53. R. A. Neimeyer, *Lessons of Loss: A Guide to Coping*, McGraw-Hill, New York, 1998.
54. T. A. Rando, *Treatment of Complicated Mourning*, Research Press, Champaign, Illinois, 1993.
55. B. Raphael, The Management of Pathological Grief, *Australian and New Zealand Journal of Psychiatry, 9*, pp. 173-180, 1975.
56. L. D. Siggins, Mourning: A Critical Survey of the Literature, *International Journal of Psychoanalysis, 52*, pp. 259-266, 1966.
57. J. D. Canine, *The Psychosocial Aspects of Death and Dying*, Appleton & Lange, Stanford, Connecticut, 1996.
58. H. Deutsch, Absence of Grief, *Psychoanalytic Quarterly, 6*, pp. 12-22, 1937.
59. G. Krupp, Maladaptive Reactions to the Death of a Family Member, *Social Casework, 53*, pp. 425-434, 1972.
60. S. Zisook and R. DeVaul, Grief-Related Facsimile Illness, *International Journal of Psychiatry in Medicine, 7*:4, pp. 329-336, 1976-77.
61. C. M. Parkes, Bereavement and Mental Illness, *British Journal of Medical Psychology, 38*, pp. 1-26, 1965.
62. C. M. Parkes and R. S. Weiss, *Recovery from Bereavement*, Basic Books, New York, 1983.
63. S. Zisook, S. R. Schuchter, and M. Schuckit, Factors in the Persistence of Unresolved Grief among Psychiatric Outpatients, *Psychosomatics, 26*, pp. 497-503, 1985.
64. B. Rapheal, *The Anatomy of Bereavement*, Basic Books, New York, 1983.
65. S. Zisook and R. DeVaul, Unresolved Grief, *American Journal of Psychoanalysis, 45*, pp. 370-379, 1985.
66. S. Zisook and L. Lyons, Bereavement and Unresolved Grief in Psychiatric Outpatients, *Omega, 20*, pp. 307-322, 1990.
67. N. Hogan, J. M. Morse, and M. C. Tason, Toward an Experiential Theory of Bereavement, *Omega, 31*:1, pp. 43-65, 1996.
68. G. A. Bonanno, D. Keltner, A. Holen, and M. J. Horowitz, When Avoiding Unpleasant Emotion Might Not Be Such a Bad Thing: Verbal-Autonomic

Response Dissociation and Midlife Conjugal Bereavement, *Journal of Personality and Social Psychology, 46,* pp. 975-989, 1995.

69. G. A. Bonanno, H. Znoj, H. L. Siddique, and M. J. Horowitz, Verbal-Autonomic Dissociation and Adaptation to Midlife Conjugal Loss: A Follow-Up at 25 Months, *Cognitive Therapy and Research, 23*:6, pp. 605-624, 1999.

70. C. R. Figley, B. E. Bride, and N. Mazza (eds.), *Death and Trauma: The Traumatology of Grieving,* Taylor & Francis, Philadelphia, 1997.

71. B. L. Green, Defining Trauma: Terminology and Generic Stressor Dimensions, *Journal of Applied Social Psychology, 20,* pp. 1632-1642, 1990.

72. H. Krystal, *Integration and Self-Healing: Affect, Trauma, Alexithymia,* Analytic Press, Hillside, New Jersey, 1988.

73. C. B. Wortman, E. S. Battle, and J. P. Lemkau, Coming to Terms with the Sudden, Traumatic Death of a Spouse or Child, in *Victims of Crime* (2nd Edition), R. C. Davis, A. J. Lurigio, and W. G. Skogan (eds.), Sage, Thousand Oaks, California, pp. 108-133, 1997.

74. E. E. Rinear, Psychosocial Aspects of Parental Response Patterns to the Death of a Child by Homicide, *Journal of Traumatic Stress, 1,* pp. 305-322, 1988.

75. L. M. Redmond, *Surviving When Someone You Love was Murdered,* Psychological Consultation and Education Services, Clearwater, Florida, 1989.

76. E. K. Rynearson, Psychological Effects of Unnatural Dying on Bereavement, *Psychiatric Annals, 16*:5, pp. 272-275, 1986.

77. B. A. Van der Kolk, *Psychological Trauma,* American Psychiatric Press, Washington, D.C., 1987.

78. J. Gyulay, The Violence of Murder, *Issues in Comprehensive Pediatric Nursing, 12,* pp. 119-137, 1989.

79. A. W. Burgess, *Rape Victims of Crisis,* Robert Brandy Co., Bowie, Maryland, 1984.

80. A. Amick-McMullan, D. G. Kilpatrick, L. J. Vernon, and S. Smith, Family Survivors of Homicide Victims: Theoretical Perspectives and an Exploratory Study, *Journal of Traumatic Stress, 2,* pp. 21-35, 1989.

81. V. M. Sprang, J. S. McNeil, and R. J. Wright, Psychological Changes after the Murder of a Significant Other, *Social Casework, 4,* pp. 159-164, 1989.

82. F. Ochberg (ed.), *Post-Traumatic Therapy and Victims of Violence,* Brunner/Mazel, New York, 1988.

83. R. A. Kulka, W. E. Schlenger, J. A. Fairbanks, C. R. Marmar, and D. S. Weiss, *National Vietnam Veteran's Readjustment Study (NVVRS): Description, Current Status, and Initial PTSD Prevalence Rates,* Veterans Administration, Washington, D.C., 1988.

84. P. Marris, *Loss and Change,* Pantheon, New York, 1975.

85. I. L. McCann and L. A. Pearlman, *Psychological Trauma and the Adult Survivor: Theory, Therapy and Transformation,* Brunner/Mazel, New York, 1990.

86. C. M. Parkes, Psychosocial Transitions: A Field for Study, *Social Sciences and Medicine, 5,* pp. 1110-1115, 1971.

87. S. Roth and L. Lerbewitz, The Experience of Sexual Trauma, *Journal of Traumatic Stress, 1,* pp. 79-105, 1988.
88. S. Roth and E. Newman, The Process of Coping with Sexual Trauma, *Journal of Traumatic Stress, 4,* pp. 279-297, 1991.
89. R. Janoff-Bulman, *Shattered Assumptions: Towards a New Psychology of Trauma,* Free Press, New York, 1992.
90. S. C. Jacobs, *Traumatic Grief: Diagnosis, Treatment, and Prevention,* Brunner/Mazel, Philadelphia, Pennsylvania, 1999.
91. S. Jacobs, C. Mazure, and H. Prigerson, Diagnostic Criteria for Traumatic Grief, *Death Studies, 24*:3, pp. 185-199, 2000.
92. R. Masters, L. Friedman, and G. Getzel, Helping Families of Homicide Victims: A Multidimensional Approach, *Journal of Traumatic Stress, 1,* pp. 101-125, 1988.
93. E. K. Rynearson, Bereavement after Homicide, *American Journal of Psychiatry, 141,* pp. 1452-1454, 1984.
94. C. M. Parkes, Psychiatric Problems following Bereavement by Murder or Manslaughter, *British Journal of Psychiatry, 162,* pp. 49-54, 1993.
95. E. K. Rynearson, Psychotherapy of Bereavement after Homicide, *Journal of Psychotherapy Practice and Research, 3*:4, pp. 341-347, 1994.
96. W. Middleton, B. Raphael, N. Martineck, and V. Misso, Pathological Grief Reaction, in *Handbook of Bereavement Theory, Research and Intervention,* M. S. Stroebe, W. Stroebe, and R. O. Hansson (eds.), Cambridge University Press, Cambridge, United Kingdom, pp. 44-61, 1993.
97. C. M. Parkes, *Bereavement: Studies of Grief in Adult Life* (2nd Edition), International Universities Press, Madison, Connecticut, 1987.
98. B. Raphael and W. Middleton, Current State of Research in the Field of Bereavement, *1st Journal of Related Science, 24,* pp. 1-2, 1987.
99. American Psychiatric Association, *Diagnostic and Statistical Manual of Mental Health Disorders* (4th Edition), Author, Washington, D.C., 1994.
100. A. Amick-McMullan, D. Kilpatrick, and H. Resnick, Homicides as a Risk Factor for PTSD among Surviving Family Members, *Behavior Modification, 15,* pp. 545-559, 1991.
101. D. R. Applebaum and G. L. Burns, Unexpected Childhood Death: Post-traumatic Stress Disorder in Surviving Siblings and Parents, *Journal of Clinical Child Psychology, 20*:2, pp. 114-120, 1991.
102. S. Burman and P. Allen-Meares, Neglected Victims of Murder: Children's Witness to Parental Homicide, *Social Work, 39*:1, pp. 28-34, 1994.
103. J. L. Dyson, The Effect of Family Violence on Children's Academic Performance and Behavior, *Journal of the National Medical Association, 82*:1, pp. 17-22, 1990.
104. R. S. Pynoos and S. Eth, Witness to Violence: The Child Interview, *Journal of the American Academy of Child Psychiatry, 25*:3, pp. 306-319, 1986.
105. C. H. Zenah and G. S. Burk, A Young Child Who Witnesses Her Mother's Murder: Therapeutic and Legal Considerations, *American Journal of Psychotherapy, 38*:1, pp. 132-145, 1984.
106. K. Doka (ed.), *Disenfranchised Grief: Recognizing Hidden Sorrows,* Lexington Books, New York, 1989.

PART ONE
Our Stories

The following ten chapters contain real stories of homicide survivors. The names have been changed but the circumstances remain the same. The survivor's own words have been used to depict his or her experience. Some of the stories are slightly graphic and may cause some emotional discomfort. These stories are typical of what homicide survivors experience. More horrific stories are heard at national Parents of Murdered Children (POMC) conventions, at National Victims Week celebrations, or seen in various grief chat rooms on the World Wide Web. The following stories are real stories from homicide survivors that I interviewed.

CHAPTER ONE
Jack

Jack is a pleasant man who loves to talk. He is 54 years old, married with three children and four grandchildren. He lives just outside a small city in a neighboring state nearly an hour from where I live. When he found out I was interested in doing qualitative research on homicide survivors he readily agreed to be interviewed, in fact he specifically asked to be included in the study. Jack felt that by sharing his story he might "help someone else." We agreed to meet half way between his home and mine at a local truck stop. Jack wore a Parents of Murdered Children (POMC) baseball cap and brought newspaper articles and pictures with him. The newspaper articles were about his granddaughter's murder and the trial that followed. The pictures were of his granddaughter Lisa. Jack was a truck driver for 17 years but is currently disabled and unable to work due to medical problems related to stress. He spends most of his time helping other homicide survivors by attending court hearings, explaining the judicial system and what the survivors can expect to happen, and by writing letters to keep perpetrators in jail for the maximum sentence allowed.

Jack's daughter's boyfriend killed his two-year-ten-month-old granddaughter Lisa in 1994. The boyfriend was watching Lisa at home while Lisa's mother was working the afternoon shift. Lisa was not the boyfriend's daughter. During the evening, the boyfriend called Lisa's mother at work to tell her Lisa was choking on something.

"He [the boyfriend] never admitted to it, he denied it from the word go, but he admitted to being the only one alone with her when it happened. He was the only one alone there when it happened and he tried to say she was choking to death on something but the pathologist, in his report, said that her [Lisa's] main artery had been ripped from her heart and her liver split in two. You're not going to get that from choking on something. He [the boyfriend] tried to say it happened from her falling on a toy three days earlier. The pathologist said with those kinds of injuries, she [Lisa] bled to death in five seconds.

I believe Lisa was kicked so hard in the stomach that her artery was ripped from her heart and her liver was spilt in two."

Jack believes Lisa was a victim of child abuse at the hand of his daughter's boyfriend.

"I didn't think about it until afterwards, but the signs of child abuse were there. One time Lisa had a bruise on her forehead and the boyfriend said 'she slipped getting into the bathtub.' It was a plastic bathtub but we didn't think much of it at the time. Lisa was very active and kids get bruised from time to time. It happens. Wednesday Lisa had bruises to her chest area that he said were from her falling on a Barney train. Saturday morning she was dead. Maybe if we had paid more attention to what was going on, Lisa would be alive today. You just don't think people hurt little children."

The boyfriend was working when he met Lisa's mother but quit when he moved in with her. Later Jack found out the relationship between Lisa's mother and the boyfriend was troubled from the beginning. Jack's daughter kept that from him so Jack would not worry.

Jack was very close to his granddaughter; although he had other grandchildren, Lisa was his favorite grandchild. She was his first grandchild and his only granddaughter at that time.

With a huge smile and sense of pride he said, "She was my little buddy."

Jack talked about how Lisa would help him tinker around the house, build the deck out back, and she always wanted to go for a ride with Grandpa.

"We were like two peas in a pod. When I went somewhere she went with me and she even liked the Cleveland Browns." Jack laughed when he mentioned the Cleveland Browns. It is unusual for a Pennsylvania resident to rally for the Cleveland Browns and not the Pittsburgh Steelers.

Jack was devastated by Lisa's death because not only did he have to deal with the loss of his granddaughter, he had to try to comfort his daughter with the death of her only child by someone she loved.

"The first six months there could *not* have been any more pain. We grieved for the loss of our granddaughter and for our daughter's loss too. We were hurting for her [daughter]. She lost her daughter and her boyfriend. She was in so much pain; it was a double loss for us. You're not supposed to outlive your kids let alone your grandkids."

The boyfriend was apprehended and charged with Lisa's murder.

"For three days he [boyfriend] let us believe she choked on something. He even acted sad up until the police came to arrest him."

Having never been to a murder trial before, Jack and his family were not prepared for what happened. They were not prepared for the attack on Jack's daughter's lifestyle and reputation.

"It's as if she were on trial, instead of the real killer. They tried to make it sound like she was some kind of prostitute or something.

"In our state [Pennsylvania] when you kill someone under the age of 12 you're supposed to be charged with first-degree murder. But this was the judge's first murder case as a judge and he was a defense attorney before that. He kept so much information from the jury and I think he confused the jury when he explained intent to kill. The jury came back with a charge of third degree murder.

"The boyfriend was given 10 to 20 years. Ten to 20 years is not enough for taking another person's life, especially a *child's* life."

Jack talked about how he believes that after the boyfriend does the 20 years in jail he will come after his daughter. He is very concerned for his daughter's safety.

"This is a kind of guy who holds a grudge. I think he'll try to kill my daughter when he gets out.

"Even after the sentencing, the boyfriend's sister threatened to cut my daughter's throat because her brother was found guilty."

Jack's anger over his granddaughter's death, the pain and insults to his family during the trial, and the lenient punishment of the perpetrator has forever changed Jack's life. Jack was determined to prevent others from experiencing the same sense of aloneness that he and his family did after Lisa's death. He joined a Parent's of Murdered Children (POMC) and Other Homicide Survivors support group and a year later started a POMC support group in his own community.

After Lisa's death, Jack describes his experience as, "At first I was in a daze. I'd walk around and wouldn't know what I was doing. I was confused. I couldn't even think straight. Nothing made any sense. You're in constant pain."

"For over a year I was at the cemetery every day. It was the only way I could cope. I just wanted to be with her.

"When I was driving a truck, I'd have to pull off to the side of the road because I was so upset when I thought about her. At a truck stop I'd find a waitress, even if she didn't wait on me, and tell her what happened. I just had to have someone to talk to, someone to listen. Later on just helping other people has helped me with my own grief."

Jack faithfully and consistently assisted other homicide survivors by attending murder trials and sitting with the surviving families in the courtroom.

"Some people say just having someone there helped them deal with their pain. Sitting through other people's trials brings back a lot of my own hurt and pain but I do not let that interfere with why I am there—to support them. I cry for other people too because I know what they went through. I *know* the pain."

Because he and his family were traumatized by the murder trail, Jack dedicated his life to helping others through their living hell. Jack traveled a tri-state area nearly every day to help other survivors. He made speeches, organized fund-raisers, and gave interviews, whatever he could do to raise public awareness and support for homicide survivors.

"My life has changed tremendously. Before I never thought about death. Now I think about it everyday. Life is not the same and it never will be. There are pictures of Lisa on the wall that will never change.

"At first I kind of blamed God. He could have stopped it. He could have struck him [boyfriend] down instead of Lisa. But I know that's not how the Lord works. He gives us all a choice and we have to pay for the choices we make."

Jack says homicide survivors need to talk about their experience, their feelings, their pain, and they need someone to just listen. He mentions that he sees a lot of families file for divorce after a murder because they do not communicate.

"One day I'd be smiling, laughing, and joking around. That doesn't mean I'm not hurting inside. The picture on the outside is different than what's on the inside. You're putting on a show because a lot of it is a show. I'm not going to say to make other people think you're feeling better but you want to be able to function with other people so you do what you think they want. A lot of people are afraid to talk about murder. It makes them uncomfortable. But married people have to talk to each other and explain that they are hurting inside although they might not be showing it. Otherwise the other person might think they don't care, that they aren't hurting any more.

"Some people don't want to open up and talk. They want to hold it in and I think that makes things worse. Their anger builds and they take it out on each other. Although you can't really know what a person is feeling, if you've gone through the same thing you have an *idea* of how they are feeling. You can somehow share their pain. You can help them realize what they are going through is normal for a homicide survivor."

Jack told me his health was failing and that he needed a heart transplant as a result of all stress of his granddaughter's murder. He said Lisa's death had "broken his heart" and that the stress of dealing with her death was just too much to cope with. When I met Jack he said he felt better than he had felt in a while but that he wanted to die, that he wanted to be with his granddaughter. Jack said he was tired and that he had done what he wanted to do by starting the POMC group in his area and now it was up to someone else to take over.

Although he was still on the waiting list for a heart, Jack felt he would not live long enough to see a transplant. His affairs were in order as much as he could get them in order [he was not eligible for life insurance because of his poor health] but he insisted he only wanted to die to be with his granddaughter. He was ready to die.

"If I died today I wouldn't care because I'd be with her. At least I hope I'd be with her. Hating him [boyfriend] so bad, I don't know if the Lord will forgive me. I don't hate him so much as I hate what he did."

Jack stated that the Victim Witness Coordinator and Police Department were very helpful during his granddaughter's murder trial. Both departments provided as much information to Jack and his family as legally permitted. The POMC support group was also helpful. Jack felt so strongly about the need for the support group that he started one in his own community.

Jack apparently had a heart attack and died while driving one afternoon. He died less than a year after I talked to him.

Notes

Path Through the Criminal Justice System

A murder case official enters the criminal justice system after a warrant is issued and a suspect is arrested or otherwise charged. Normally the first appearance a suspect makes before a court after an arrest is at arraignment where the suspect is advised of the nature of the charge(s) against him or her, legal representation is assured, and bail may be set. Most people who are thought to commit a crime are arrested in order to ensure that they will appear at trial. If a defendant can assure he or she will appear at all pre-trial hearings and the trial if released, he or she is entitled to reasonable bail or conditions of release. Bail may be in the form of cash or other property. If the defendant posts bail then fails to appear for any hearing, the cash or property is forfeited to the state or federal government and an arrest warrant is issued.

The case may be considered by a grand jury. The grand jury is a panel of citizens who hear and review the state's evidence against the accused person in a closed hearing. They determine what charges will be pursued and the charges may be different from those of the original arrest. The purpose of the grand jury is to determine if there is enough evidence to take the case to trial. Testimony is secret and usually does not become part of the public record.

There may be several pre-trial and other court hearings before the actual trial. One of these may be a suppression hearing in which the defense challenges part or all of the state's evidence. Usually the only testimony in a suppression hearing is by law enforcement personnel.

Another hearing that may occur is a competency hearing. This usually follows a psychiatric examination of the defendant and involves medical testimony to determine if the defendant is mentally competent to understand the nature of the charges.

There could also be a motion for discovery, which means the prosecution and defense share information such as physical evidence and witnesses. Real trials rarely have surprise witnesses.

Following the pre-trial hearings, the case is ready to go to trial. The defendant, however, may elect to enter a plea of guilty to a charge. This means there is no trial. A brief statement of facts is read into the court record as well as a summary of any consideration (deals) offered for the plea. Generally, a defendant may plead guilty or no contest. A no contest plea means that the defendant does not challenge the factual allegations but may not be willing to admit guilt or may want to preserve some issue for appeal. After a no contest plea, the judge determines guilt. The judge makes a finding.

A trial may be before a judge or before a jury, or in some states, before a three-judge panel. When a trial is held, the prosecution presents evidence and testimony. The defense then presents testimony and evidence on behalf of the defendant. The defendant is never required to testify, but may do so. After all the evidence is presented, the judge or jury then deliberates until a decision is reached. In most states a jury's decision must be unanimous. If the jury cannot reach a decision, it may be declared "hung" and a new trial may be scheduled before a different jury. Every state has time limits within which a defendant must be brought to trial, but the process may take six to nine months to complete. Delays are common practice.

Sentencing is usually the last action of the trial court. Following a conviction, the presiding judge imposes punishment. A judge will have some discretion, but for the most part the minimum and maximum length of a sentence is set forth in the criminal code of each jurisdiction of the court.

During the sentencing hearing, the defense may make a statement noting mitigating factors that could be considered in lessening the penalty. The prosecution may also make a statement giving the position of the state. The offender is permitted to make a statement. Many states also allow the survivors to speak at the sentencing hearing. This would be in addition to any written statement presented.

Sentences may be as little as a few days in the county jail or as severe as a death penalty. At the time of sentencing, offenders are given credit for any time served prior to the trial. A jail sentence may also be suspended and the offender placed on probation.

At the time of sentencing, the offender may be ordered to pay reparation or restitution. Reparation usually refers to burial expenses, while restitution refers to out-of-pocket expenses sustained by the survivor as the result of property loss or damage and medical expenses.

All convicted offenders have the right to request an appeal. This means a higher court or appellate court can review the entire case. The state can never appeal a not guilty finding. The defense submits a written brief noting the areas where an error may have occurred. The prosecution is then given an opportunity to respond. These documents, along with a transcript or video of the trial, are submitted to the appellate court for review. There may be an oral argument before the court, but no new evidence or testimony may be presented. The appellate court affirms or overturns the trial court decision. If the conviction is overturned, the case may be retried.

After review by an appellate court, the case may then be taken to the state supreme court and later the U.S. Supreme Court. An appellate court and usually the state supreme court automatically review cases involving the death penalty. The case may be subject to several additional levels of review called "post conviction relief" [1, 2].

Infanticide

According to the U.S. Department of Justice Bureau of Justice Statistics, the number of homicides of children under age five increased over the past two decades but has declined recently. While the incidence of infanticide has increased, the rates have remained fairly stable. Infanticide rates for Black children have fluctuated, but are currently lower than in previous years. Infanticide rates for White children have remained stable and infanticide rates for children of other racial groups have declined. In 1999 the homicide rate for children under the age of five was 2.2 for Whites, 7.4 for Blacks and 2.0 for Others per 100,000 populations [3, 4].

From 1997 to 1999 the homicide of children under 5 five dropped from 350 in 1997 to 331 in 1999 for Whites and 260 to 237 for Blacks [3].

Of all the children under age five killed in 1999, 30 percent were killed by the mothers, 31 percent by fathers, 23 percent by male acquaintances, 6 percent by relatives, and 3 percent were killed by strangers. Of the children killed by other than parents, 82 percent were killed by males [3].

Parents of Murdered Children (POMC)

Parents of Murdered Children (POMC) is dedicated to the idea that grief must be shared. It is the only national helping organization that is specifically for the homicide survivors and it follows up with supportive family services. POMC was founded by Reverend and Mrs. Robert Hullinger after their daughter, Lisa, then 19, was bludgeoned to death by an ex-boyfriend.

Mrs. Hullinger says, "Most people don't have any idea what it's like to have a child murdered."

POMC provides ongoing emotional support to facilitate the reconstruction of a "new life" and to promote a healthy resolution. POMC helps survivors deal with acute grief as well as the criminal justice system. The National headquarters of POMC will assist any survivor and, if possible, link that survivor with others in his or her area who have survived a loved one's murder. POMC is available to provide individual assistance, support, and advocacy. They also help anyone interested in starting a POMC chapter in their local area.

POMC provides training to professionals in law enforcement, mental health, social work, community service, religion, media, and mortuary affairs in the areas of homicide survivors and the aftermath of murder.

POMC local chapters hold monthly meetings, provide a telephone network, supply information about the grieving process, organize a speaker's bureau, and provide accompaniment for survivors who attend court hearings. Many chapters publish their own newsletters outlining their activities and involvement in the community.

Most meetings begin with introductions of each survivor telling of his or her loss. Often there is a topic to guide discussion such as the grief process or the court process. Usually meetings revolve around group members' own knowledge and experiences, but occasionally outside speakers are invited to present information and to learn from survivors.

As members help one another by sharing experiences, feelings, and insights, and by allowing others to do the same, their grief is somehow lessened. POMC provides an opportunity for survivors to share stories, thoughts, and feelings, without judgment or admonishment. The support group provides for a safe outlet and expression of grief [2].

Endnotes

1. David Betras, Attorney-at-Law
   P.O. Box 177
   114 East Front Street
   Youngstown, OH 44501-0177
   330-746-8484
   http://betrasmarucakopp.com
2. Parents of Murdered Children and Other Homicide Survivors
   100 East Eighth Street
   Cincinnati, OH 45202
   1-888-818-POMC
   http://www.natlpomc.com
3. Bureau of Justice Statistics, *Reports to the Nation on Crime and Justice,* U.S. Department of Justice, Washington, D.C., 1999.
   http://www.ojp.usdog..gov/bjs/ homicide/children/htm
4. Federal Bureau of Investigations, *Crime Index Trends, January through June 2000,* U.S. Department of Justice, Washington, D.C., 2000.
   http://www.fbi.gov

CHAPTER TWO
Miriam

Miriam is a 60-year-old woman full of energy. She works in the Prosecutor's Office as a Victim Witness Program Coordinator. She is married and has 12 children. She lives in the city and walks a few blocks to work each day. Her husband is a retired civil servant. Miriam has snow-white hair and caring blue eyes. She is very patient and listens intently to what you have to say. She firmly believes in supporting homicide survivors but not enabling them. She explains enabling as allowing the homicide survivor to "wallow in self pity."

Miriam started the first Parents of Murdered Children (POMC) and Other Homicide Survivors support group in the area shortly after her son was killed. Her story is so well known and horrific that to this day people call her from all over the country for help in dealing with their own personal tragedies. She says she has letters from all over the world asking for help dealing with the personal tragedy of murder. As recently as February 2001, a local television station interviewed Miriam about how she dealt with her son's tragic death.

Her work with homicide survivors and the POMC support group led her to her current position as a Victim Witness Coordinator. At first she was a volunteer helping homicide survivors go through the legal process and deal with their pain; eventually she was hired full time by the prosecutor's office.

In 1985, two teenage boys murdered Miriam's 12-year-old son Raymond.

"My son was 12 years old. He was on his way to his friend's house to go to a Boy Scout meeting together. He was taken off his bicycle, beaten and raped, strangled and sodomized with a broom handle, mutilated, and then set on fire.

"When Raymond didn't show up at his friend's house we went to look for him. They looked for what seemed hours. My husband found him. He was just barely breathing and managed to survive for two days without regaining consciousness. Because there were no brain waves, they disconnected him. He died.

"I remember when this happened I ran screaming. I was the one that stayed home that night while everyone was out looking. I was to stay by the phone in case someone called. I received a phone call from my son-in-law saying that they found him, that he had gone to call an ambulance, and that my husband stayed with our son. I remember just going completely hysterical running from the house to the neighbor's house telling them 'something had happened to my baby and I needed to go there. I needed to go where my husband and son were.' The young man across the street took me to the crime scene. When I got there I saw ambulances and everything and I felt I shouldn't go back there where he was because I wasn't going to be able to do anything while they were working on him except perhaps get in their way and be hysterical. I knew that I had enough sense to know that I would be of no help.

"Then I started hyperventilating. I was lucky that someone happened to have a bag in their car and I think I used that bag a good 45 minutes just breathing in because it seemed I couldn't breathe any other way. Eventually my husband and I followed the ambulance to the hospital.

"At the hospital I kept saying 'I don't want to see him, I can't see him knowing those things that they did to him.' I kept saying, 'I can't see him. I want to remember him the way he was.' At the time they already did the EEG and it didn't look like much hope for him. I was paranoid at that moment. I did not want to see him in that condition. I just wanted to remember him the way he was. Then my husband came to me and said, 'Maim you're going to have to see him.'

"I didn't want to go in the room because if I didn't go in and see him, he wouldn't really be gone. I didn't want to face the reality of his death. But I knew I had to, I had to because they say that people that are unconscious can sometimes hear you and I had to let him know that I was there and that he was still my baby and I loved him.

"To prepare me to see Raymond, my husband had the hospital staff cover my son; they turned him this way [flat on his back with his face to the right], covered him up to his neck so that the only part of him that I could see when I went in was his face. I mean when you walked in to see him you would think he was just a young child lying asleep because he had no bruises or marks on his face except a little scratch. His hair was still beautiful. The hospital staff cleaned him up and you could not tell the damage to his brain by the perpetrators beating him repeatedly on the back of the head.

"I remember seeing the burn marks around Raymond's neck where they strangled him.

"It wasn't our choice to disconnect Raymond; it was the doctor's decision. That really took a burden off of us. The choice was out of our hands. The guilt was not on us.

"It's a horrible feeling to know that your child is out there being tortured and you're not there to help in any way. If I had been there and had been beaten or something else, I still would have felt like I wasn't able to do anything.

"One of the hardest things I had to hear in the courtroom was the confession of one of the boys. He stated that he was standing watch while the other boy was doing his number on Raymond, raping him etc., and somehow or another my son got away from that boy and came running out and thought this young man would help him, not realizing he was part of the game. He [Raymond] said to him, 'Please take me to my mother. I have to go to a Boy Scout meeting. Please take me to my mother.' And when I heard that in the courtroom, it was just like I had dreamed. I had dreams that Raymond was crying out for me. I think that was one of the worst times in the trial that I had to go through. It was the only time that I had to leave the courtroom because I cried uncontrollably. I couldn't help it. I could not stop crying."

Miriam has 12 children; not counting the children she used to board at her house for other families who could not afford to take care of their own children. Raymond was the youngest of the 12. Miriam talked about how Raymond loved to argue points with her and that she told him he would make a great lawyer one day because of his logical arguments.

Raymond was active in school sports and Miriam keeps his trophies and other mementos in a box in the attic. Miriam says Raymond was extra special because he was not a planned child.

"When I found out I was pregnant with Raymond, it was like 'what do we do? We have all these children and we're poor but we work and we're providing but one more is going to take more away from them and what do we do?' My husband and I considered an abortion and we even talked to a counselor. We discovered that abortion was not in the cards for us. It was not something we could do. We just said 'we'll manage to feed one more' and we had Raymond."

Miriam and her husband made do as best they could for their family and those they cared for by taking on second jobs when necessary.

"I remember, and these things add to your bereavement as far as I'm concerned, two people, elderly ladies, coming into the funeral home when Raymond died. They were one of the first people in line, and I didn't know either one of them. They just came in to view him because they read so much in the paper about what had happened to him. I remember the ladies stepping around the corner being one of the first ones in the room. Of course you know when you stand there in line waiting for people to come pay their respects to you, it's like you're very tense and the anticipation of what you're going to go through emotionally is very great. These two women stuck their head around the corner and said, 'Aw, they have a closed casket,' and they turned around and walked out of the funeral home. They just came to see the damages done to Raymond, to see what torture looked like. Those kinds of things stick with you and they have a lot to do with how you grieve because you think of the people that are insensitive to what happened to you and your family."

Both Raymond's killers were apprehended. Both had records of assault before they attacked and killed Raymond. One boy had two violent rapes about a year and a half before he killed Raymond. He was sentenced to juvenile detention for the rapes. He was there for a year; until he turned 18 then he was released.

"He was a vicious, vicious person. Before they caught him for murder, he got a girl from the middle school during lunch hour and raped her in broad daylight, 12 noon.

"The other young man, the 17 year old that was involved in Raymond's death was a very vicious and violent homosexual.

"These two people happened to come together that night in the parking lot of a store and just happened to see my son coming in a distance through the field on his bicycle. They decided in just one split second what they were going to do. We should not of had two individuals out there like that."

Unlike Megan's law pertaining to adult sexual predators, juvenile predators are not required to be listed with local authorities. They do not have the same restrictions and reporting procedures.

The one killer was sentenced to death row and the other was sentenced to life in prison.

"I have been strength to a lot of people and that is to me is a consolation. If you ask people to remember the victims who have been murdered in the past 10 to 15 years, they're always going to remember Raymond because I won't let them forget he was a person. I won't let them forget the fact he was such a young child and that a lesson should be learned about how we watch our children and our concern about them going places by themselves. Sometimes we think its broad daylight and it's fine to allow a child to go through a field or go somewhere. We are not aware of some of the kinds of animals that are out there and I hate to use the word animals because animals are kinder than these human beings [killers] were."

Miriam believes that there are lessons to be learned from even the most horrific circumstances and once the lessons are learned, they should be shared with others so that maybe they can prevent or ease someone else's pain. She freely shares her experience and the lessons learned from that experience—professional and personal experiences. She advocates listening to and sharing experiences as ways to ease the pain of murder.

Notes

Victim Witness Program

Generally a Victim Witness Program (VWP) is a program developed so that crime victims and witnesses to crime receive fair and compassionate treatment while participating in the criminal justice system. The VWP helps victims by providing emotional support, practical aid, and advocacy. The VWP has two goals. The first is to reduce the psychological shock and trauma a victim suffers by lending immediate emotional and practical support at the crisis scene or shortly thereafter. Studies have shown that if a victim receives support at the time of or shortly after a crisis, psychological trauma is greatly reduced, thus speeding the re-establishment of some sort of normalcy in the victim's life.

Second, the VWP aims to help the victim after the initial crisis with emotional support, counseling, advocacy, referral to local social service agencies, and where possible, information on the status of the investigation, the status of the accused, the court system and the victim's rights within the court system, safety, security, and much more.

Typical Victim Witness Program services include:

- Courtroom assistance such as courtroom tours, confidentiality forms, closed circuit televisions, closed preliminary hearings, interpreters, criminal justice process support and explanation, accompaniment to court, and trial preparation assistance;
- Financial assistance such as travel and meal reimbursement, restitution, referrals to social services, and property return;
- Victim impact such as victim impact statement and preparation of parole input, right to remain in courtroom, and prosecution liaison;
- Notifications of court dates, release of prisoners, notice of appeals and habeas corpus, case status information, employer intercession, and status of bond;
- Protection such as protection orders, separate waiting rooms, escort services, referral to community services, and safety planning; and

• Support services such as 24-hour on-call crisis intervention, hospital support, crisis referrals, and emergency assistance.

Services vary in each state. Contact your Victim Witness Program for more information in your area.

Victim Impact Statement

The Victim Impact Statement is usually completed at the same time as the presentence investigation and should address the physical, mental, and emotional injury suffered by the survivor. In some jurisdictions, a form is provided to the survivor while other jurisdictions complete a statement in a personal interview.

A Victim Impact Statement allows the homicide survivor to write about the physical, emotional, and financial effects of the murder, as well as any other changes they may have experienced. If the defendant pleads guilty or is found guilty after a trial, the Victim Impact Statement helps the judge understand how the murder has affected the survivor and those close to them.

The survivor's statement will become an official court document after it is given to the court and it will become part of the defendant's permanent file. The judge, prosecutor, and probation officer will read the statement. Prison and parole officials may read the statement if the defendant is sentenced to a prison term. The defendant and the defendant's attorney will also be able to read what has been written. The defense attorney may ask the survivor questions about the statement in court.

Center for Victims of Crime's Victim Services

Another service available to the homicide survivor is the National Center for Victims of Crime's Victim Services. They have a toll free telephone service (1-800-FYI-CALL) that offers immediate referrals to the closest, most appropriate services in the victim's community.[1] The National Center refers victims to services such as crisis intervention, research information, assistance with the criminal justice process, counseling, and support group information. The National Center's INFOLINK generates sustained victim advocacy. In addition to providing referrals and information on emotional, physical, and financial implications of victimization, the staff may also contact key individuals in the victim's community to discuss the case, identify

[1] The INFOLINK Bulletins can be ordered by calling 1-800-FY1-CALL or downloaded from their Web site at http://www.ncvc.org/infolink/main.htm.

specialized counseling or support services, forward legal research, or provide specialized information to local victim service providers.

INFOLINK bulletins cover a wide-range of topics including domestic violence, homicide, sexual assault, workplace violence, female offenders, victims' rights, and a host of other legal issues.

Megan's Law

Every state has enacted some version of "Megan's Law," named for a seven-year-old New Jersey girl who was raped and murdered in 1994 by a paroled sex offender who moved into her neighborhood. The Megan laws generally provide for some type of public notification of the whereabouts of convicted sex offenders after their release from prison.

Under the law, an individual found guilty of kidnapping, rape, involuntary deviate sexual intercourse, aggravated indecent assault, or some prostitution and obscenity offenses is referred to a state board before sentencing. The board makes a recommendation to the trial judge about whether the offender is a "sexually violent predator." The trial judge holds a hearing, at which the burden rests on the offender to prove by "clear and convincing evidence" that the designation is unjustified.

Those who are designated as sexually violent predators face a possible maximum sentence of life in prison, mandatory life term if convicted of another sex crime, and/or stringent registration requirements if they get out of prison.

CHAPTER THREE
Sue

Sue is a married 50-year-old woman. She lives in a small town in a rural community with her husband of 28 years. She has her own business cleaning homes and she drives two hours each way to watch her granddaughter two nights each week while her daughter works. I met Sue at her house on her day off. She was very emotional while telling her story and she had to stop to cry then regain composure several times during our meeting.

Sue's 17-year-old daughter, Stacey, was murdered by her boyfriend's friends. Stacey's boyfriend Tommie was killed at the same time. Sue had several pictures of Stacey on the walls throughout the front room and the hallway of her home. The pictures were at various stages of Stacey's life until she turned 17.

"Tommie had been doing drugs and must have been out selling them the night they were killed. We gather that Stacey drove my car to where Tommie was going to sell the drugs. When they got there, Stacey and Tommie were pulled out of the car by three guys and were put into a yellow Cadillac. After driving around for a while, they all got out of the car. They shot Tommie four times in the head. Stacey must have tried to run because they shot her in the leg and later shot her in the back of the head."

Sue talks about how she did not care for Stacey's boyfriend Tommie. He was three years older than Stacey was and he was "half-black."

"At first he seemed like a nice kid but he got involved in drugs. Tommie also tried to get Stacey involved in drugs and may have succeeded."

Sue said she tried to get them to break up several times but Stacey insisted she loved Tommie. She said that Stacey was the kind of girl who thought she could get Tommie to change and get away from the drugs. At one point, Sue decided that since nothing else had worked to break them up she had to get tough with Stacey and told her that if she loved

Tommie so much then he could support her. She locked Stacey out of the house and insisted she live with Tommie.

Afterwards Sue remembers one day Tommie called her asking for money. She told him, "You should have thought about that before you turned my daughter into a tramp. Until she's out of your life I don't want her anymore and you can lose my phone number."

Since Tommie was not working, Sue thought Stacey would quickly grow tired of supporting her boyfriend and would come home. One night Stacey and Tommie had a big fight, and Stacey decided to go live with her older sister. On her way to her sister's house, Stacey was involved in a serious car accident. She fell asleep at the wheel and the car she was driving hit the tires of a tractor-trailer that was driving next to her car. Miraculously, Stacey walked away with only minor injuries.

A few days after the car accident the driver of the truck called Sue and told her that Stacey "must have a guardian angel watching over her because there was no way she should have survived the accident. He was certain divine intervention saved her life that day."

When Sue learned of the accident, she allowed Stacey to come back home. Sue described her relationship with Stacey as tense and often strained but six weeks before she was killed, Sue said she and Stacey were getting along quite well.

She said, "I remember at one point Stacey said she didn't want me to tell her that I loved her anymore, that it embarrassed her in front of her friends. The day she died, I remember standing by the sink with my back to the door. Stacey was on her way out the door. I almost said I love you, but I said 'Stac have fun hun.' And then she was gone. I wanted to tell her that I loved her but I didn't. I should have."

"To this day, I regret not saying it. I wish I'd said 'I love you' because in one of those ugly moments I kept saying he [Tommie] was going to get her killed because that's what I felt. She'd say I was crazy or whatever. I said, 'Stacey, with your dying breath you're going to think, my God, Mom was right, he did get me killed.'

"Damn I miss her and I wish I had appreciated our time together. It's like I wasted our time together. It wasn't important that she cleaned up her room; instead we had to have words. Instead of sitting down watching a movie or eating popcorn we had to fight.

"We went to a movie the night she was killed. Around 10:30 a cold chill ran over me and I thought she's in trouble. When my husband and I got home there were about 20–30 hang up calls on the phone. Later we realized that word of Stacey's death was already on the streets.

"At about 12:15 we got a call from the hospital. The woman told us to come down to the emergency room that Stacey had been shot. When I asked if she was alive she said she couldn't tell me anything over the phone. I literally hit the floor. After my husband picked me up off the floor, I called Tommie's mother and told her to find Tommie.

"When we got to the hospital we were told Stacey was dead. When we finally got to see her there was yellow tape around her gurney, the kind that says caution or police on it. We were told we couldn't touch her because we might *contaminate* the evidence.

"The hospital staff had cleaned her up. They'd taken a bullet out of her forehead. You could see where the bullet hole was butterflied back. You could also see the terror in her eyes. It must have been hell for her to see Tommie shot and his face fly off.

"I am convinced that if she had lived she would have tried to kill herself. She wouldn't want to live after seeing Tommie killed. We would have had to institutionalize her to keep her from killing herself. She was so in love with him.

"Tommie's mother never got a phone call about Tommie being killed; no one recognized him because they shot his face off. When she found out about Stacey, she went to the hospital and found Tommie's body herself."

Sue talked about how the media complicated matters by hounding her and her family almost immediately, wanting all the gory details.

"I was so devastated that I couldn't even make a complete thought and these vultures were wanting the gory details the next day. They came to the house to see me sobbing—what's newsworthy about that?

"I cried every day the first year. When I was by myself I would be sobbing, I couldn't think of anything else.

"I let Stacey start dating Tommie when she was 15; it was the worst thing I could have ever done. I no longer beat myself up about that. I had to let that go. You have to move on because you can't take back what you've done. You can't change things.

"The last year of trying to get her away from Tommie, life was hell. We didn't say too many nice things to each other. I don't regret trying. If I hadn't tried so hard to break Stacey and Tommie up, I wouldn't be able to live with myself today.

"My husband has trouble today because he left all that up to me. He's hasn't dealt with the whole thing. He just keeps it locked away."

Three men were arrested within a week of Stacey and Tommie's murder but it took two years to convict them. Two men were sentenced to two 15–to life terms and the other man was sentenced to seven years in prison.

Sue believes her network of friends helped her through the difficult times of coping with her daughter's murder.

Notes

POMC Identifies 27 Problems of Homicide Survivors.

1. Isolation, helplessness in a world that is seen as hostile and uncaring, and that frequently blames the victim;
2. Feelings of guilt for not having protected the victim;
3. The memory of a mutilated body at the morgue, how much did my love one suffer?;
4. Getting back the personal belongings of a murder victim;
5. Sensational and/or inaccurate media coverage;
6. Lack of information;
7. Endless grief;
8. Loss of ability to function on the job, at home or in school, etc.;
9. The strain on marriages (frequently resulting in divorce), and the strain on family relationships;
10. Effects on health, faith, and values;
11. Effects on other family members, children, friends, co-workers, etc.;
12. Indifference of the community, including professionals, to the plight of survivors;
13. Society's attitude regarding murder as a form of entertainment;
14. Financial burden of medical and funeral expenses;
15. Medical expenses for stress-related illnesses and professional counseling for surviving family members;
16. Financial burden of hiring private investigators, etc.;
17. Public sympathy for murderers;
18. The feeling that the murderer, if found, gets all the help; homicide survivors have few rights;
19. Outrage about the leniency of the murderer's sentence;
20. Disparities in the judicial system (frequently punishments for property crimes are as great or greater than the crime of taking a human life);
21. Anger over a plea bargain arrangement/agreement;
22. Frustration at not being allowed inside the courtroom at the time of the trial;
23. Unanswered questions about the crime—What happened?;
24. Unanswered questions about postponements and continuous delays throughout the trial;
25. Bitterness and loss of faith in the American criminal justice system;
26. After conviction, the long appeals process begins; and

27. Constantly reliving your story through the dreaded parole process.

Endnote

POMC Web page – http://www.pomc.com/problem.html

CHAPTER FOUR
Ray

Ray is a retired, chain-smoking, 60-year-old man. He's very active in POMC. He has been on the radio and television talk shows advocating support for homicide survivors. He also gives presentations to local schools on the affects of drugs and alcohol. I met Ray at his home in the suburbs of a small city. He showed me pictures of his daughter Sharon and her son. After his daughter Sharon was killed, Ray and his wife raised her son as their own.

Ray is very articulate and very passionate about the injustice he and his family suffered over his daughter's death. His 20-year-old daughter was murdered by her boyfriend in 1978. It took 16 years before someone would declare Ray's daughter's death a murder.

"You could see where she had been beaten over the head. You could see the bruising on the side of her face; her face was swollen tremendously. Her lips were swollen to the point they were turned inside out. I saw fingerprints on her neck then I said, 'Oh God, she's been beaten.'"

Ray's daughter, Sharon, had recently given up her life of alcohol and drugs. She had found peace in religion and dedicated her life to helping others. She tried to get her friends to convert also.

Ray talks about how one night Sharon got a call from her ex-boyfriend. She turned pale and took the phone in the other room, which was something she ordinarily did not do. After the call Sharon asked her father for $2600. When he asked what for, she explained that her ex-boyfriend needed it. Ray knew her ex-boyfriend was still dealing drugs so he would not give the money to Sharon. In fact he insisted she was not to have anything to do with him because he was nothing but trouble. Sharon tried to explain to her father that the ex-boyfriend was not going to like that answer, but Ray insisted that "was too bad." Sharon said she would have to get the money somehow. Ray told her the ex-boyfriend would have to find somewhere else and that she should stay away from him.

Ray said Sharon promised him that she would not go see the ex-boyfriend, but some time during the night Sharon snuck out of the house and met with the ex-boyfriend. When Ray got up in the morning he noticed Sharon was not in her room. He thought she went out early in morning as she sometimes did. That evening when she still did not come home and the family had not heard from her all day, Ray called the police.

The following day, a police officer came to the house to tell Ray Sharon was dead. The police told him that she died of an apparent drug overdose. Ray insisted that was not true because Sharon was not doing drugs anymore, but the police officer explained they found drugs near her body. Ray said he cried so much and so hard that the next day he had sore eyes and a sore throat.

Word got to Ray that the ex-boyfriend wanted to see Sharon's body at the calling hours. Ray left explicit instructions with the funeral director not to let that happen because he felt the ex-boyfriend had killed her. Ray even had family members posted at the funeral home to ensure that the ex-boyfriend did not get to Sharon. On the day of the funeral, Ray and his family decided to leave early for the funeral home. When they got there they saw the ex-boyfriend at the back of the funeral home with the funeral director.

"I couldn't believe what was going on. I almost lost my mind."

Ray confronted the funeral director about disregarding his wishes and was told, "This is a public place and I didn't think it would hurt anything." Ray told him to call the police because if the ex-boyfriend did not leave immediately there was going to be a fight. The ex-boyfriend left without incident. Ray and the funeral director had words about the incident but the pain and disrespect had already been inflicted.

Sharon died in August. That first Christmas, four months after Sharon's death, Ray and his family prepared for the holiday as they usually did expecting friends and family to visit, but they did not. No one showed up.

"Friends and family didn't know what to say; they didn't know what to do. We were alone."

They did not celebrate. The lack of support from family and friends adds to the grieving process. Ray explains that the holidays are really hard for him and his family because the holidays were celebrated as a family and Sharon is no longer around to celebrate with them. Her son is a constant reminder that she is gone. Ray explains that it is not necessarily the day (holiday or birthday) that is so hard to cope with as it is the week before.

"Just thinking about it and anticipating that day to come becomes very stressful and depressing."

A year went by and Ray felt like he was "still going out of my mind." He was still going to the cemetery before and after work everyday looking for answers, looking for peace. He went to the police, the prosecutor's office, and the newspapers, and they all told him they would not do anything.

After six years, Ray's health started to deteriorate. He was in and out of the hospital a dozen times but he said he felt he "couldn't give up trying to prove Sharon was murdered and not a victim of a drug overdose."

Ten years after Sharon's death a local newspaper did a five-day story on how the police bungled investigations in the area. Ray called the paper to ask why they did not mention his daughter's murder. The reporter he talked to had no idea what Ray was talking about and was interested in what he had to say.

The reporter met Ray and his family. They got hold of some of the police records and ran a story in the newspaper.

Shortly after the newspaper story, the prosecutor decided to reopen Sharon's case. Ray's family "went through living hell for 16 years" because no one wanted to hear what Ray had to say or look at all the facts. The newspaper article raised too many questions for too many people. Sharon's body was exhumed and tests were ordered. Within a week Ray and his family were told Sharon was choked to death, that she had been murdered and not overdosed on drugs as had been declared 16 years earlier.

The investigation was slow and discouraging for Ray and his family.

"The prosecutor's office was uncooperative and the Sheriff's office had destroyed some of the evidence."

During the trial the prosecutor "gave the ex-boyfriend's wife a hug and said 'I'm sorry for what you're going through.'"

The Sheriff department was put on alert before the verdict was read.

"For the first time in the history of the court house 70 deputies were standing by at the end of the trial."

When a not guilty verdict was read, Ray and his family were ordered to leave the courthouse by the Sheriff's department, "You guys get the hell out of here or we'll put you under arrest." The family was threatened with arrest at their own daughter's murder trial.

The television station that was taping the trial later reported that after the verdict was read, the judge shook the hand of the ex-boyfriend.

"It was as if the case was decided before it ever even went to trial. It was a mockery of the whole justice system.

"There was nothing else I could do. I went on talk shows and told my story. I had nothing to lose anymore. It was a travesty of justice; 16 years of living hell."

Ray said the justice system treated his daughter like garbage because she did have a problem with drugs earlier in her life but she was beyond that when she was killed.

"She was still my little girl. I'll never give up those 20 years I had with her. I have good memories of her and I won't let the bad memories sour me.

"I wish her friends would understand where I am and would talk about Sharon but I can see they are very uncomfortable. They don't know what to say or they are afraid it will upset me."

Ray and his wife raised 11 children over the years, including three adopted children, three foster children, and Sharon's son. They try to help "throw away" kids just as "Sharon would have."

Ray and his wife also attend trials with other homicide survivors, providing moral support and some explanation of the judicial system. Ray explains to survivors that although taking a plea bargain is not what the survivor may want to happen, the killer is likely to spend time behind bars and that is better than nothing.

"A lot of people think the judicial system is great. Until something like murder happens to them, people don't find out just how rotten the system really is."

Notes

Homicide Survivor Rights

It may appear that the court system is set up to favor the accused, but homicide survivors do have rights. Almost all states and the federal court system have enacted statutes addressing the rights of victims and several states now have constitutional amendments that compliment and strengthen the statutory law.

Most importantly, victims have the right to be treated with dignity and respect. As a homicide survivor, a person has the right to be notified of all pre-trial and trial actions. If the survivor is not a witness, he or she has the right to attend any or all of these hearings. If the homicide survivor is a witness or is otherwise needed to testify, he or she may not be allowed to sit in the courtroom during some of the hearings.

Expect court personnel to be sensitive to the survivor's needs and if they aren't, court personnel should be reminded that this is very difficult for all involved. Contact the victim advocacy program. If there is no program, contact the prosecutor's office and find out who is handling the case. Make an appointment with the prosecutor and take a list of all questions. Demand answers.

Medical Examiner/Coroner

As required by law, the death of a loved one must be reported to the medical examiner or coroner of the jurisdiction where the deceased is pronounced dead, or where the body is found. This may not be where the offense occurred. It is the medical examiner that determines that the death was not of natural causes and will perform an autopsy. The purpose of an autopsy is to determine the cause of death and to independently document any trauma suffered by the victim.

By law, the medical examiner is authorized to order an autopsy without obtaining a signed consent by the next of kin. In most jurisdictions, however, an attempt will be made to contact the family and advise them of the need for an autopsy.

Once a death has been reported to the medical examiner, the remains of the deceased come under the control of the medical examiner or coroner. The body will be transported to the medical examiner's office. At this time, the survivor should choose a funeral home. Once the funeral home has been selected, funeral home personnel will work directly with the medical examiner and the body will be released to them.

Most medical examiners or coroners will allow the survivors to view the body during normal working hours, especially if the family has not had an opportunity to say good-bye.

Personal effects have to be held by the investigating agency as evidence. The police agency or prosecutor handling the case will decide what can be released and when.

Autopsies

Autopsy means "see for yourself." It is a special surgical operation, performed by specially trained physicians, on a dead body. Its purpose is to learn the truth about the person's health during life, and how the person really died.

A pathologist is a physician with a specialty in the scientific study of body parts. This always includes a year or more learning to do autopsies. A coroner is a political position elected by voters, while a medical examiner is a physician, usually a pathologist. Exactly who makes the decisions and who just gives advice depends on the jurisdiction. Autopsies can be ordered in every state when there is suspicion of foul play. In most states an autopsy can be ordered when there is some public health concern such as a mysterious disease or a worry about the quality of health care. In most states, an autopsy may be ordered if someone dies of undetermined reasons or the attending physician is uncomfortable signing the death certificate.

When a loved one dies, a family can ask the hospital to perform an autopsy. The hospital pathologists are supposed to be independent and there is no connection between them and the clinician that treated the patient. This service is usually free.

If the family prefers, a private pathologist can do the autopsy in the funeral home. It does not much matter whether the body has been embalmed first or not.

Whoever does the autopsy, there should not be a problem with an open-casket funeral afterwards. This is true even if the brain has been removed and the dead person is bald. The pillow in the casket will conceal any marks left by the autopsy.

If the law does not require an autopsy, the legal next-of-kin must sign an autopsy permit. An autopsy is done with respect and seriousness. The pathologist first examines the outside of the body. The body is opened using a Y-shaped incision from the shoulders to mid-chest and down to the pubic region. If the head is to be opened, the pathologist makes a second incision across the head, joining the bony prominence just below and behind the ears.

The pathologist uses a scalpel for these incisions. There is almost no bleeding since a dead body has no blood pressure except that produced by gravity. The incisions are carried down to the skull, the rib cage and breastbone, and the abdominal cavity, which contains the organs of the abdomen. The scalp and soft tissues in front of the chest are then reflected back. The pathologist looks for abnormalities.

The skull is opened using two saw cuts, one in front and one in back. These cuts will not show through the scalp when it is sewn back together. The top of the skull is removed and the brain is very carefully cut free of its attachments from inside the skull.

When the breastbone and attached rib cartilages are removed, they are examined. Often they are fractured during cardiopulmonary resuscitation (CPR). Freeing up the intestine takes some time. The chest organs, including the heart and lungs are inspected. Sometimes the pathologist takes blood from the heart to check for bacteria in the blood. Sometimes the pathologist will send blood, urine, bile, or even fluid from the eye for a chemical study and to look for medicine, street drugs, alcohol, and/or poisons.

Then the pathologist must decide in what order to perform the rest of the autopsy. The choice will be based on a variety of considerations. One method, Virchow, removes the organs individually and examines them closely. When the internal organs have been examined, the pathologist may return all but the portions he or she has saved for further study to the body cavity or the organs may be cremated without being returned. The appropriate laws and the wishes of the family are obeyed.

The breastbone and ribs are usually replaced in the body. The skull and trunk incisions are sewn shut ("baseball stitch"). The body is washed and is then ready to go to the funeral director.

The pathologist submits the tissue he or she saved to a histology lab to be made into microscopic slides. When these are ready, the pathologist will examine the sections, look at the results of any lab work, and draw his or her final conclusions. A final report will be ready in a month or so. The glass slides and a few bits of tissue are kept so that other pathologists can review the work [1].

Victimization

The United States is ranked first of all developed nations in the number of homicides [2]. Murder or non-negligent manslaughter is defined as intentionally causing the death of another person without extreme provocation or legal justification [3]. In the United States over 24,000 people are murdered each year and over 2 million people are injured in rapes, robberies, and assaults. About 1 in 3 victims of violent crime suffer from some form of physical injury [3]. The homicide rate doubled from the mid-1960s to the late 1970s. In 1980, the homicide rate peaked at 10.2 per 100,000 population and subsequently fell off to 7.9 per 100,000 in 1985. The rate rose again in late 1980s and early 1990s to a peak of 9.8 per 100,000 in 1991. Since then, the homicide rate has declined, reaching 6.8 per 100,000 in 1997. The murder rate declined 1.8 percent the first six months of 2000 compared to the same time period in 1999 [4].

The number of homicides where the circumstances were unknown has more than doubled since 1976. Homicides resulting from arguments have declined but remain the most frequently cited circumstance for murder. Homicide committed during the commission of another felony such as robbery or burglary has fluctuated. Homicide involving adult or juvenile gang violence has increased five-fold since 1976 [5].

Homicides are more likely to involve multiple offenders than multiple victims. The percentage of homicides involving multiple offenders increased dramatically in the late 1980s and early 1990s, increasing from 10 percent in 1976 to 16 percent in 1999. The percentage of homicides involving multiple victims increased gradually during the last two decades from just fewer than 3 percent of all homicides in 1976 to 4.5 percent in 1999 [5].

Homicides are most often committed with handguns. Like the homicide rate generally, gun-involved incidents increased sharply in the late 1980s before falling recently. During the same time period, homicides involving all other weapons have slowly declined. In 1999, 7950 homicides involved handguns, 2049 involved knives, and 903 involved blunt objects [5].

The southern regions historically have had higher homicide rates than other regions of the United States. Rates of murder, especially those involving guns, are higher in Southern regions of the United States, in the South Atlantic, East South Central, and especially the West South Central regions. Higher than average rates are also found in the Pacific region. Relatively low rates of homicide exist in the New England, Mountain, and West North Central regions of the United States. Homicide victimization rates of cities with a population of 1 million or more have plummeted to the lowest level in the last two decades; cities with populations of 250,000 to 499,999 are equivalent to the homicide rates of the largest cities. The rates of the largest cities, 500,000 to 999,999, fell below the rates for cities of one-quarter to one-half million population; cities with populations of 100,000 to 249,000 are the lowest homicide rates among the larger cities.

In 1999, 18- to 24-year-olds experienced the highest homicide offender rates at 27.7 per 100,000 population. This was a change from the late 1970s when 25- to 34-year-olds had the highest rate. In 1999, homicide victims rates were at 20 per 100,000 for 18- to 24-year-olds. Homicide offender rates for the same age group were 30 per 100,000 populations.

Males are most often the victims and perpetrators in homicide. Males are 3.2 times more likely than females to be murdered. In 1999, rates for both males and females reached the lowest point in two decades. Blacks were six times more likely than Whites to be murdered. Blacks were seven times more likely than Whites to commit homicide.

For the years 1976–1999 combined, among all homicide victims, women were particularly at risk for intimate and other family killings, sex-related homicide, and murder by arson or poison [5].

From 1976 to 1999, Whites killed 86 percent of White victims. Blacks killed 94 percent of Black victims. While 38 percent of interracial murders involved offenders under the age of 25, one half of the interracial killings involved younger perpetrators. Stranger homicides are more likely to cross racial lines than those that involve friends and acquaintances.

Homicide survivors are repeatedly victimized by the action of the defendant (if any) or the legal process because of the legal stratagems employed by the defense to cast doubt on the victim. Other examples of the victimization include intrusions of the media, insensitivity of the prosecutor, the lengthy process of the criminal justice system, the callousness of the police, and lack of understanding of friends and family members. The legal system presents a difficult obstacle and often revictimizes the homicide survivor [6-10]. The criminal justice system can be a lengthy intrusive process and does not always produce the results for which the survivor hopes.

The National Organization for Victim Assistance [cited in 11] identified four common reactions of survivors of violent crimes: isolation, blame, stigmatization, and injustice. These reactions embody revictimization (or secondary victimization). Many homicide survivors insist that such victimization is in many ways worse than the murder itself because it occurs by those that the survivor expects to help them and protect their rights [2, 8, 10, 12].

Homicide survivors are often unprepared to deal with the police, the criminal justice system, and the media; as a result, they feel victimized a second time [13].

Besides dealing with the death of a loved one, the homicide survivor is forced to cope with the reality of victimization from various agencies the survivor looked to for support. The realization of the victimization often leads the survivor to withdraw from society. Although the withdrawal is often looked on as pathology, I suspect it is a necessary part of coming to terms with the death of a loved one. Withdrawing allows the bereaved an opportunity for self-reflexivity, which I argue, is a normal part of the homicide bereavement process.

References

1. E. Friendlander, Homepage, *Autopsy*. Retrieved January 3, 2000 from the World Wide Web: http://www.pathguy.com/autopsy.htm.
2. R. J. Meadows, *Understanding Violence and Victimization*, Prentice Hall, Upper Saddle River, New Jersey, 1998.
3. J. H. Laub, Patterns of Criminal Victimization in the United States, in *Victims of Crime* (2nd Edition), R. C. Davis, A. J. Lurgio, and W. G. Skogan (eds.), Sage, Thousand Oaks, California, pp. 9-26, 1997.
4. Federal Bureau of Investigations, *Crime Index Trends, January through June 2000*, U.S. Department of Justice, Washington, D.C., 2000.
5. Bureau of Justice Statistics, *Reports to the Nation on Crime and Justice*, U.S. Department of Justice, Washington, D.C., 1999.
6. A. W. Burgess, Family Reaction to Homicide, *American Journal of Orthopsychiatry, 45*, pp. 391-398, 1975.
7. J. Gyulay, The Violence of Murder, *Issues in Comprehensive Pediatric Nursing, 12*, pp. 119-137, 1989.

8. L. M. Redmond, *Surviving When Someone You Love was Murdered,* Psychological Consultation and Education Services, Clearwater, Florida, 1989.
9. V. M. Sprang, J. S. McNeil, and R. J. Wright, Psychological Changes after the Murder of a Significant Other, *Social Casework, 4,* pp. 159-164, 1989.
10. C. B. Wortman, E. S. Battle, and J. P. Lemkau, Coming to Terms with the Sudden, Traumatic Death of a Spouse or Child, in *Victims of Crime* (2nd Edition), R. C. Davis, A. J. Lurgio, and W. G. Skogan (eds.), Sage, Thousand Oaks, California, pp. 108-133, 1997.
11. E. E. Rinear, Psychological Aspects of Parental Response Patterns to the Death of a Child by Homicide, *Journal of Traumatic Stress, 1,* pp. 305-322, 1988.
12. T. A. Rando, *Treatment of Complicated Mourning,* Research Press, Champaign, Illinois, 1993.
13. M. Bard and D. Sangrey, *The Crime Victim's Book,* Basic Books, New York, 1979.

CHAPTER FIVE

Mike

Mike is a 30-year-old man who works as a night shift dispatcher for a local police department and part-time for the city water department. Being a bit leery of a stranger, Mike wanted to meet me at a local coffee shop rather than at his home. He was anxious to be part of my research. He brought three large binders, a videocassette, and an 8 × 10 picture of his brother with him. Mike was very eager to talk and it was obvious he had told his story many times.

Mike's 22-year-old brother Butch was killed by his best friend in 1988.

"They [police] believe Ed had a gun. They believe that he took his gun and hit Butch in the head with it. Probably knocking him unconscious. Ed and his brother then restrained Butch's hands behind his back with a pair of handcuffs. They had his legs tied together with a necktie. Then they broke every bone in his face and head by smashing it against pipes that were there at the gas well. They beat him up, stuck a garbage bag over his body, and threw him in the back of the car. The guys then buried Butch's body behind the farmhouse."

Butch was an athlete and he liked sports. His roommate Ed was interested in marital arts. Both were going to college and they both worked out together at the gym that was owned by a doctor. The doctor owned a lot of businesses around the community. Linda was the doctor's mistress and business manager. Linda was younger than the doctor, but older than Ed and Butch. Linda and the doctor were also half owners of a furniture store.

Linda started dating Ed and she got him and Butch a job. Ed worked at the furniture store and Butch did the advertising for the furniture store as well as the doctor's other businesses.

At one point Ed talked Butch into taking some things from some guys at the college fraternity house where they both stayed. Ed was an officer in the fraternity so he had keys to the fraternity house and all the rooms.

"Ed had this idea to go there and take some things and convinced my brother not to worry about it because these guys had insurance on this stuff and they'll turn it in to their insurance company and get brand new stuff."

Ed and Butch got away with the burglary. Then Ed and Linda asked Butch to help burn down the furniture store warehouse for the insurance money.

"We believe that my brother felt bad enough after stealing from the fraternity house that he wouldn't help them burn the warehouse down and told them so."

Because Butch would not help burn the warehouse down, Ed got his brother and another guy to help him. The three of them set a fire and burned the warehouse to the ground. Within two weeks the warehouse was leveled, cleared off, and gone.

The authorities thought the fire was suspicious so they started questioning all the employees. By that time Butch had already graduated from college and moved home. The police went to his hometown and started asking him questions about the fire and about the burglary at the fraternity house. Butch broke down and admitted to the burglary and agreed to turn himself in. Linda and Ed found out that Butch was going to turn himself in for the burglaries and they were afraid he would turn them in for burning the warehouse down.

"The next thing we knew Butch was planning to go to visit two girls he'd just met from out of town. He went on the bus and I stood at the door and watched him leave. That was the last time I saw him.

"The two girls met him at the bus station. Supposedly Ed and Linda talked these girls into getting my brother to meet with them. For whatever reason they conned them into doing it. The plan was for the two girls to meet Butch at the bus station and take him to a secluded area near a gas well without telling him why.

"The day Butch was due to arrive Linda went to Ed's brother's girlfriend's house and waited. The two guys went to the gas well and waited.

"The girls picked up Butch at the bus station and took him to the gas well. The plan was that the two girls would sit next to each other so that Butch would be next to the door. The girls drove to the spot, Butch got out of the car, the girls suddenly slammed the door shut, and took off.

"As the girl that was driving later testified, as they were driving off, she glanced in the mirror and she saw Butch down on the ground and the guys were standing over him. The two girls did not go back to the gas well and that supposedly was the end of their involvement.

"The police believe Ed had a gun and that he hit Butch in the head with it, hard enough to put a hole in his skull. Ed and his brother beat Butch, put him in a garbage bag, and threw him in the back of the car. They claim he was dead then but we don't know for sure.

"The guys drove to where Linda was waiting and then they went to a farmhouse. After the guys buried Butch outside, they went in the farmhouse to clean up. Before they left there the guys realized they had not removed any identification from Butch's body so they dug him up and removed his wallet. They then buried the carpet from the car, which was covered in blood, with him.

"Testimony was given by Linda that Ed 'was laughing and acting real proud about what he did as he was washing Butch's blood from his body.'"

When Butch did not come home for a couple days, his mother called the girls and they told her Butch never showed up. Butch was known to change his plans suddenly without telling anyone so at first his mother was not too concerned but after four days she called the police. Eventually detectives went to talk to the girls and they told them the same thing, that Butch never showed up to meet them.

"A year went by and one girl got married. The other girl started dating Ed and Linda got jealous."

Meanwhile Mike and his family were searching the countryside for Butch.

"Mother tells us of the fraternity house burglary after he was missing and about the warehouse burning down because she's worried those people did something to Butch.

"Linda found out Ed is about to get married and she becomes a scorned woman. She hired a couple of unemployed homeless men to burn her new house down while she went on vacation with her new boyfriend. The detectives thought the fire was suspicious, especially after Linda's warehouse burnt down a year earlier. When questioned by the police, Linda told the detectives that she thought Ed burnt her house down and that Ed killed his best friend. She even showed the detectives where Butch was buried."

Ed was arrested, his brother was arrested, and eventually Linda was arrested. The two girls were also arrested later on.

"The detectives got a hold of my dad and told him of the body and that it might be Butch's so he came to the house to tell my mother. 'I wanted you to know they found this body and it might be his but they don't know for sure. They have to do an autopsy and compare dental records.'

"It was kind of weird because earlier that same day when I came home from work I checked my answering machine and I had gotten call from a neighbor and she said, 'I heard they found your brother.' And I thought why would this lady call me and tell me this. Why wouldn't I have heard this from my mother or father, or my sister, or the police? I thought yea right, she's an older lady, maybe she has this mixed up with another case or maybe it was something else. Later on as I'm cleaning the furnace, the phone rings and it was my mother and she tells me they may have found Butch's body.

"'What should I do now? I live alone. I don't have anybody to tell this to.' I went to my neighbor's house but she wasn't home so I went to my uncle's house to talk to someone.

"The next day I go to work. All day long I kept thinking 'well they think that it was him so maybe it is not him, it's not, it's someone else.' When I finished my shift, my boss came over to me and said, 'Mike I got a phone call from Channel 27. They want to come down here and do an interview with you, something about they found your brother.' I told him, 'I didn't want to do an interview at work.'

"I called my mother and she hadn't heard anything either. 'They're hounding me here. They're calling from all the television stations; they're coming to the door, all the media is here. They won't leave me alone.'

"I went down to mother's house. People kept coming to the house knocking on the door, calling on the phone. It was my job to deter these people. I asked them 'to leave us alone right now. We don't even know if that's him and we're hoping it's not him. If we find out later that it is him and we want to talk to you we will but for now leave us alone. We don't want you to make us keep thinking it was him. We hope he's still alive somewhere.'

"The media was bad at this point. They went to our neighbors' homes knocking door to door asking what kind of people we were, to see if we were white trash or bad people. They would see people on the street corner and ask them if they knew us. They were looking for dirt because they didn't get any information from us."

The family waited for the identification results for several days before they got a call from the hospital. When they got to the hospital they were not allowed to see Butch's body. The coroner told them dental records had positively identified the body and they could not see it. The funeral home picked up the body and told the family the casket was sealed and it could not be opened. It was not until the second trial where pictures of Butch's body were shown that the family got to see Butch's body. That was two years later. Mike could only recognize the shoes Butch had on because he had just bought them before he disappeared and Mike remembered what the shoes looked like.

Mike searched for his brother the whole time he was missing. At first it was everyday in the city where Butch went to meet the two girls. He put up posters, talked to the police department, the sheriff department, and the state's attorney's office. He said he even searched through dumpsters in back alleys, just looking for something that might belong to his brother. Every time he had a day off or any extra time, he spent it looking for his brother. During the year-long search for his brother, Mike said he received calls from all over the country reporting sightings of Butch, but they turned out to be crank calls. He never gave up hope. He never stopped looking.

There were five people involved in killing Mike's brother. Two of the women who were least involved pled guilty after they were caught. They were given suspended sentences and they had to testify against the other three perpetrators. The two girls were student teachers that just graduated from college. They had to forfeit their teaching certificates as part of their sentence. The other woman, Linda, was sentenced to 7 to 15 years because she was not convicted of murder but rather conspiracy to commit kidnapping.

"She was the mastermind behind the whole thing. She was an older woman and she manipulated these other people into this scheme. But because she was not with the two brothers when they killed my brother, she could not be convicted of the actual murder."

The two men were sentenced to life in prison.

Mike says he lost some of his friends while dealing with the death of his brother.

"They were supportive while we were searching for my brother and until the funeral but after that, they said it was 'too depressing.'" One friend in particular told him he was, 'Making her sad all the time' just thinking about my brother.

"My 'friends' weren't there for me. On the weekends they'd go to the club or the dance hall but I needed them to be with me. They weren't there. They didn't want anything to do with this court business or this death business. They thought that once the funeral was done, that everything else was over.

"The Victim Assistance Program coordinator became my second family during the trials. We'd have lunch or dinner together. I even stayed over at her house when I couldn't get a hotel for the trial. Other than that, there was no one."

Mike believes in the death penalty because "it shows society that there are consequences for crimes and punishment serves as a deterrent. If the murderer goes to prison instead, they are still allowed to live and they got away with murder. Some sentences are minimal then they are set free but the dead person (victim) is still dead."

Mike's story was made into a movie. He and his family were consulted during the production so that the movie might reflect the actual circumstances as closely as Hollywood allows it to be and still sell. Mike keeps a copy of the manuscript (and the video) in a binder along with the other two binders related to his brother's death. The binders contain news clippings, pictures, etc.—things related to Butch's death.

Like many other homicide survivors, Mike spends time in the courtroom helping other homicide survivors get through the judicial system.

"Sometimes when you hear about what others have been through, your situation doesn't seem quite so bad. I learned as I went along, the hard way. Prior to all this I didn't even know what a prosecutor was or what he or she did. Now I have the opportunity to help others."

Mike initiates petitions to keep his brother's killers in prison for their maximum sentence. He even attends the parole hearings so that he can testify in person about how his brother's murder has affected his life and that of his family. So far, the killers are still in prison. They have not been granted parole, although some have met the parole board more than once.

Mike advocates education as a good way to help homicide survivors. Mike said his learning process, although a difficult one, helped him understand the judicial process that was totally unfamiliar to him prior to his brother's death.

Notes

Parole

Parole should not be considered as an award of clemency or a reduction of sentence. The granting of parole allows a person to serve the remainder of his or her sentence in the community under supervision, subject to various rules and conditions imposed by the parole board. With the exception of those individuals sentenced under a death penalty statute, most offenders are considered for parole at some point. Rather than releasing inmates from prison without controls, parole provides for the gradual reintegration of the offender in the community.

Most parole boards function as independent and autonomous structures of the executive branch of government. Parole eligibility is usually established by statute but allows some discretion of the parole board. The scheduling of a parole hearing does not necessarily lead to the release of the offender. The parole board will consider the seriousness of the offense for which the individual has been convicted, the offender's past arrest record, and adjustment while in the institution. Parole boards also consider the Victim Impact Statement. Mike's input to the parole boards has prevented parole for Linda, Ed, and Ed's brother.

A notification system is in place in most parole departments, which allows for the notification of all scheduled hearings to victims and survivors. It is usually incumbent upon the homicide survivor to tell the parole board of the wish for information concerning the offender. Shortly after sentencing, send a short, written note to the parole authority telling them of the wish to be notified of hearings. If an address changes, send the new address. The only way a parole department can notify the survivor(s) is if he or she keeps them advised of the current address. After receiving notification of a hearing, the survivor may respond in writing, stating his or her feelings, appear in person before the parole board, or take no action. Offenders are usually paroled to the state and county of their residence—that is not necessarily the state and county where the offense occurred.

POMC Parole Block Program

For homicide survivors, the early release of convicted murderers is seen as a denigration of their loved one and results in extremely intensified emotions. The Parents of Murdered Children, Inc.'s Parole Block Program strives to give survivors a sense of control, as well as a positive outlet for their anger, frustration, and disillusionment with the criminal justice system. PBP allows homicide survivors to participate in the parole process by attempting to keep murderers behind bars for their minimum sentence, thus protecting society from potential repeat offenders.

At the request of the survivors, POMC will write and circulate petitions to stop the parole or early release of their loved one's murderer. The petitions are sent to people across the United States. PBP does not lobby for longer sentences, but asks that the sentences imposed by the courts be served in full. Anyone, regardless of age or voting status, may sign the petition.

Since it's inception, 634 convicted murderers have been denied parole through the Parole Block Program. Names of the murderers denied parole are listed on the POMC web site at http:/www.pomc.com/denied.cfm.[1]

In 1999, the average maximum sentence length for murder was 20 years and 11 months. The average maximum time served was 9 years and 2 months—44 percent of the actual sentence. Twenty-nine

---

[1] POMC Web site: http://www.pomc.com.

percent of parole discharges returned to prison were reincarcerated for murder [1].

Reference

1. Bureau of Justice Statistics, *Reports to the Nation on Crime and Justice,* U.S. Department of Justice, Washington D.C., 1999.

CHAPTER SIX

Ron, Jean, and Kim

Ron is a 40-year-old man married to Jean and Kim is their 25-year-old daughter. Ron works as a butcher in a slaughterhouse. Jean and Kim are housewives. I met Ron, Jean, and Kim at Ron's house in a nearby state nearly an hour from where I live. All three were very emotional when discussing the murder.

Ron's house is a shrine to his son. There is a huge picture of him on the dining room wall. The television cabinet has one side filled with mementos that belonged to Ron's son.

Ron's 28-year-old son, Ronnie, was shot and killed one evening after two men robbed him in 1995.

"Ronnie was making a deposit for the store where he worked. As the night manager that was his responsibility. Two Black men came up to Ronnie's car in front of the bank and jumped in. They told him to drive. They drove up to the park. After they got there, they told Ronnie to run; then they shot him in the back. The robbers bragged about it afterwards. They planned everything including killing someone. Ronnie was going to the bank after the store closed. He called the bank before he left so they knew he was coming. They had surveillance cameras in the parking lot. The robbery is on the surveillance cameras, but there was no one inside to watch the cameras. What is to say, if there was someone inside watching that screen, they could have stopped him from losing his life that day."

The family got a call from the police to go to the hospital because Ronnie had been shot. They did get to see him at the hospital.

"He had tubes in him and his chest was all cut open. We weren't prepared for that. It was a shock. They did an autopsy, we didn't want it but it's the law with a murder case."

The first year was very difficult emotionally.

"I'd talk about it and sort of build up an immunity. You'd go from the real to not real.

"At first we were mad. We declared war on the murderers. They were not going to get away with this."

"I would have killed them if it weren't for my family. Some of my friends would have helped too. I was mad enough to kill them.

"The system let me down. The evidence was there—written and taped confessions but the jury voted by emotions 11 to 1. 'What else do you need?'"

The second trial did not have a confession but the second perpetrator was implicated in the first trial.

"You take life for granted until something like this happens. Because you don't think it's going to hit home. You hear it on the news everyday but you think it'll never happen to you, and when it does . . . ," Jean turned away to hide her tears.

Kim says, "The pain will never go away; you just have to accept it and it takes time, a lot of time."

"He was my brother. It wasn't a nobody to me. He meant a lot to me. I'd give everything to have him back. I'd give my legs if I could have my brother back." She said she meant she would literally have them cut off if it meant her brother would be alive again.

Ron continues, "His car is down in the garage. We had it repainted and paid it off. The police cut pieces from some of the seats to check for fingerprints. They pulled out the locks and had to break into the trunk. They had to bust everything in it to get in it. There was about two thousand dollars worth of damage all together."

"After they killed Ronnie, the killers rode around for a little bit in his car. But we got it fixed up. I go down there and wax it sometimes and sit in it. I get in there and get a hold of the steering wheel and just think. The car may never get used but it will always be there. It's all we got left—just memories.

"The holidays we spend at the mausoleum. It starts out as a good day. You have good intentions of having a good time. Then toward midday we all meet at the mausoleum. We sit in front of that marble wall and it's just like pulling the plug out of a bathtub. Everything goes down the drain. You walk out of there and you don't even feel like it was a holiday. You still have the rest of the family but you spend it right there. Your day has been spent. It's not fair to the rest of the family but you go through it and you more or less fake it along.

"It's just like now, the boys will be up in the garage or we'll go to a gun bash or something. It's so nice to be with them but it still hurts because there's one boy missing."

Kim adds, "At the support group [POMC] it's easier to talk than compared to anywhere else. At least at the support group everyone else in the room has gone through the same thing. They know what you're feeling and they're not going to say, 'Ok it's about time to get over it now, or quit talking about it.' Other people just really don't care anymore. They hear so much and it's like they've had enough of it. They shy away from talking about the murder because they are afraid it will bring up bad memories. But there are times when you want to talk about it and other times when you don't. But if you want to talk about it, you need to talk about it."

"Murder has no race. It has no age. There's no prejudice in murder. Whether you're black, white, green, purple, pink, or blue. Whether you're two years old, 70 or 90 years old. Murder happens.

"Nothing will make the pain go away. Nothing is going to bring Ronnie back. If the murderers were eliminated, it might make things easier, but the pain will still be there."

Ron admits, "Before Ronnie was killed I didn't pay attention to laws or the judges. Now I read letters to the editor, look at the decisions made by the judges, how they pass sentences, and how strict they are. Now I meet with the judges and ask them about their decisions."

Ron has become politically active after his son's murder. He monitors the legal issues around the death penalty and how judges, senators, and congressmen vote on the issues. He checks voting records before he votes for any political office.

He watches gun control issues also but says, "It's not the guns that kill people. People kill people." Both Ron and Kim said they now carry a gun with them at all times.

Ron and his wife Jean have also started a POMC group in their community. They say talking to someone who does not criticize them or judge them has helped ease their pain.

Notes

Policy Changes

After Ronnie died, the place of his employment at the time of his murder changed deposit procedures. A security officer now accompanies the manager to and from the bank when making deposits.

Civil Recourse

Could the death have been prevented? After a criminal trail and conviction there may be civil recourse that can assist in answering that question.

The circumstances of the offense (when, where, who, and why) dictate what, if any, avenue of compensation may be available. For example, if the victim was a guest at a hotel, a student in a college dormitory, or a passenger on public transportation, there may be a legal duty imposed on those owning and/or operating the facility to protect the person in their charge from criminal attacks. If a duty to protect against the criminal conduct can be established, then there must be evidence that there was a failure to provide the required protection that directly resulted in the victim's death.

The laws, whether statutory (enacted by Congress or state legislature) or case law (developed and established through written decisions over the years), can vary from state to state and the results under the same facts in one state may differ dramatically from that of another.

All states have time limits within which a lawsuit for personal injury or death may be filed. The effect of these limitations is that if the lawsuit is not filed in the appropriate court of law within the required time period, the claim can be forever barred regardless of the merits of the case. Although a civil case is normally determined after the criminal action, it is important to have an attorney specializing in personal injury law review the facts of the case.

Compensatory damage that may be recovered as the result of the negligent or intentional conduct of another also varies from state to state. Damages may range from financial loss incurred such as medical bills or burial expenses to damages for intangible items such as mental anguish, grief, and loss of companionship.

In addition to compensatory damages, punitive damages may also be recovered under limited circumstances. Punitive damages are assessed against the criminal or responsible party as punishment for their conduct. The fact that a criminal has been punished through the criminal justice system does not prohibit an award of punitive damages. The financial condition of the criminal or wrongdoer is directly relevant to the amount of punitive damages that may be awarded.

Types of Homicide

Maxfield [1] describes various types of homicide. Conflict homicide generally results from an argument. Instrumental felony homicides are a result of other felonies such as robbery or sexual assault, while property homicide is a result of burglaries and other such crimes. Drug homicides are considered a result of drug activities and gang homicides result from gang-related activities. These homicide types reflect the risk-related patterns of different lifestyles and routine activities [1, 2]. Often when a person is murdered while involved in a suspicious activity, the victim is blamed for his or her own murder. The homicide survivor also becomes a victim of the projection of blame by the criminal justice system.

References

1. M. G. Maxfield, Circumstances in Supplementary Homicide Reported: Variety and Validity, *Criminology, 27,* pp. 671-695, 1989.
2. R. Block and C. Block, Homicide Syndromes and Vulnerability, *Studies in Crime Prevention, 1,* pp. 61-87, 1992.

CHAPTER SEVEN
Amanda and Angie

Amanda is a 40-year-old woman with four children she is raising on her own. She works as a social worker at a local hospital. I met Amanda at a local restaurant after she finished work. Her children had soccer practice so we had two hours to talk.

Amanda's 42-year-old husband, Ben, was shot in the face while allegedly being robbed of crack cocaine in 1992.

"I received a call from the hospital asking if I was Mrs. Amanda So-and-so. I was then told that my husband was involved in an accident. I went to the hospital alone, thinking he was in a car accident, and I was cussing him the whole way there. I just knew he wrecked the car and we couldn't afford to get it fixed. When I got to the hospital, I was asked to go into a separate room. The ambulance driver is the one that told me that my husband was shot in the face and expired. There I was there by myself. I just lost it."

A man was apprehended for killing Amanda's husband, Ben, but was released after six months in jail. Ben's murder was ruled contributory misconduct in the eyes of the law.

"The killer walks the streets."

Amanda explained that her husband had a drug addiction when he came back from Vietnam. He went to rehabilitation, got sober, and even became a minister in a church. Eventually, however, Ben had a relapse and was back on the drugs.

"I had a lot of support the first few days. Ben was killed on Saturday and his funeral was Wednesday. That following weekend, Labor Day weekend, my support system fell to the wayside. Nobody knew what to say; nobody knew how to react so they didn't say or do anything. I felt abandoned."

At the time of Ben's death, Amanda's children were 7, 8, 15, and one in college. She applied for victim compensation while the police were doing their investigation. She soon found out there was a two-year waiting period.

"I was denied compensation because Ben's death was considered contributory misconduct. I appealed the decision but I was denied again. In my mind, there was never an issue about Ben's murder being a crime. He was murdered in cold blood.

"The appeal process is what kept everything stored up; it kept me from really dealing with what was going on. If the case were solved I'd have some sort of closure in that area but the case wasn't solved, it was just dismissed. That's when it hit me all over again. Ben's life wasn't considered worth an investigation or murder charge or anything because he was involved in drugs. His life was just dismissed, as if he never existed. No one thought enough to consider he had a wife and four children at home that were hurting, that he once was a decent loving human being that just had a drug problem. It wasn't as if he was this bad, evil person. He just had an addition problem."

Amanda was denied all forms of victim compensation because her husband's death was considered contributory misconduct.

"I took two weeks leave after Ben died then I gave two weeks notice. I just couldn't go to work. I couldn't do anything. It was months before I could cook. The house was a disaster. If I went out at all, it was to do some shopping. I just didn't want to be there. I didn't want to get out of bed. I didn't want to deal with life. A couple months after Ben's death my sister asked when was I going to get over it? She thought she was trying to be helpful.

"People just don't understand. You don't *get over* murder.

"At the end of the first year I decided I had to do something. I decided to go back to school. I felt like a teenager. I had no clue what I wanted to do; I had no sense of direction. I had trouble studying and concentrating. I had to read everything real slow and then I had to read it several times, even then I didn't always get what I just read.

"For two years I couldn't drive down the highway where Ben was killed. I'd take the long way around town just to avoid that road.

"It took a couple months before my seven year old cried. The older one refused to cry. He would not let it go.

"After the first two years I started dealing with Ben's death. Grief becomes a matter of choice. You decide how to deal with it. I allow myself to go back there and be sad but I control it, it doesn't control me.

"I think the time factor of dealing with one's grief is different for everyone. And a lot depends on one's support systems.

"Homicide survivors aren't pathological, as many counselors would have you believe. They are pretty normal considering what they have to go through.

"Grief is about having to adjust to a new normal. For me, I had to pull myself together and decide what am I going to do with the rest of my life. What is it that I want to get out of life?

"It's hard. When I start to feel like I'm unraveling I take some St. John's Wort herbal supplement. They say it's supposed to help calm you.

"I always had my faith. At first I was mad at God. I didn't speak to him and let him know that. I'd fall to sleep reading my Bible. I had nowhere else to go for answers or for peace so I went back to the Bible.

"I still have questions, about the meaning of life, what do I want to do with my life, and things like that. All I ever wanted to be was a wife and mother. Ben and I did everything together. We were on the same page of life our whole relationship.

"I was devastated when he started doing the drugs. I started to grieve the relationship then, but I still had hope that he would quit. He did before and I knew he could do it again. My life was shattered when he was killed. Not only was I robbed of my husband and the father to my children, I was robbed of hope. Hope that life would get better and things would go back to the way they were before the drugs.

"Now I take one day at a time."

Amanda is very involved in her children's lives.

"I would like a relationship, I miss that but I don't have one and I'm not sure how the kids would react. I don't want to upset them but I would like a relationship. I miss that. I pray and I wait. 'How do you know when it's okay to date again? How much time has to pass so people won't talk bad about you if you decided to date someone?'"

Angie is a 24-year-old girl living in her mother's house with her younger sister. Although Angie agreed to talk to me, she was a bit reluctant to do so. She did not think she had much to offer and was concerned about what her friends might think if they found out she talked to me. Some of her friends have criminal records.

Angie's first experience with murder was when she was a freshman in high school. A girl named Laura had been Angie's friend since junior high school. The girls constantly did things together after school and during the summer. Laura and Angie were 15 years old when Laura was killed.

"Laura was not from the hood, she was a normal girl. It was Halloween and we all wanted to go to a party. Laura came to the house to go with us but I missed her by one second. I yelled for her as she drove away but she didn't hear me. I thought we'd catch up with each other later on or the next day but we didn't.

"The next day her mom called asking if I'd seen Laura and that she thought that it was strange that she didn't take her purse with her wherever she'd gone. Laura was the kind of chick that didn't go anywhere without her purse. Not even for a walk down the street, that girl took her purse everywhere so I knew something was wrong.

"We later found out some 17-year-old kid slipped some acid in her drink at a party, took her to his house, raped her, and left her dead in his house for a couple days. Then he and some relative of his dropped her body off in the lake. They got caught because someone saw them dumping her body in the lake.

"The actual cause of death was ruled death by choking on her vomit but you could see bruises on her nose and mouth as if someone held her mouth shut while she was choking or screaming. Of course you'll die if you're choking and someone holds your mouth shut.

"That was in 1991. The 17 year old was sentenced to juvenile detention. He was released when he turned 18 years old."

After Angie moved into the "hood" or started hanging out with guys from the hood, death became a regular thing.

"It [murder] sucks but it's life when you live that life. Everybody knows that if they live that life style it'll happen sooner or later.

"Life in the hood is different than anywhere else. These kids grow up without a mom or dad to give them stuff, without someone that cares about them. Nobody cares about half those kids. You have to get stuff however you can.

"I block it out 'coz I don't want to remember. I don't have any feelings any more about death. You get used to it. I deal with it with alcohol and drugs.

"Three or four people that were important in my life have been murdered and I know a lot more people that have been murdered. Everybody from the hood is either dead or in jail and I'm not trying to meet any one with a life like that any more. Now they've got to have a JOB, a real legitimate job.

"Within the last couple years three people I know have been killed. Corn was shot in the street in broad daylight. He got shot 18 to 22 times, mostly in the back. His boys put 40s [40 ounce bottles of beer] on the cop outline where he was killed. We drank one for Corn before his funeral. T-Dog got shot twice, one bullet went through the back and out his stomach, and the other in his butt. He got shot at an after hours bar/restaurant when he was going to his ride. Sherman got shot in the back of the head. Someone just walked up behind him and popped him. His brains were everywhere at some crack house on the south side.

"No one gets arrested in those types of murders. Everyone knows who did it, but no one cares. 'It's just another black man dead.'

"You live to die; there's no other point. You go to school, reproduce, work, and things like that but you're going to die. That's why I live for the moment, drink and smoke. I'm going to die anyway."

Regardless of someone's life style, no one deserves to be murdered. Each time a murder occurs, someone is left behind in pain. Society does not always acknowledge that even the worst of people are loved and missed by someone when they are killed.

Amanda feels her strong religious beliefs were helpful to her after her husband was murdered. Unfortunately Angie turned to alcohol and drugs to help her cope with the multiple murders of her friends and acquaintances.

Notes

Cases Solved

The percentage of homicides cleared by arrest had been declining until recently. In 1999, 69 percent of all homicides were cleared compared to 79 percent in 1976 and 66 percent in 1993. Homicide has the highest clearance rate of all serious crimes. Clearance rates vary according to the age of the victim; homicides of children are most likely to be cleared. Law enforcement agencies clear or solve an offense when at least one person is arrested, charged with the commission of the offense, and turned over to the court for prosecution. Law enforcement agencies may also clear a crime by exceptional means such as when an identified offender is killed during apprehension or commits suicide [1].

Victims of Crime Act of 1984 (VOCA)

The Crime Victims Fund was established by the Victims of Crime Act of 1984 (VOCA) and serves as a major funding source for victim services throughout the country. Each year, millions of dollars are deposited into this fund from criminal fines, forfeited bail bonds, penalty fees, and special assessments collected by U.S. Attorney's offices, U.S. Courts, and the Bureau of Prisons. These dollars come from offenders convicted of federal crimes not from taxpayers.

All 50 States, the District of Columbia, and the U.S. Virgin Islands receive VOCA compensation grants. A state is eligible to receive a VOCA compensation grant if it meets the criteria set forth in the program guidelines. Examples of such criteria include providing services for federal crime victims and assisting victims who are victimized within the state when the victim resides in another state. Under the 1996

Antiterrorism Act, states must also provide compensation to residents who are victims of terrorist acts within or outside the United States.

The formula for VOCA compensation grants to states is based on a percentage of state payments to crime victims in a previous year.

Every state administers a crime victim compensation program. These programs provide financial assistance to victims of both federal and state crimes. Although each state compensation program is administered independently, most programs have similar eligibility requirements and offer a comparable range of benefits. Maximum awards generally range from $10,000 to $25,000.

The typical state compensation program requires victims to report crimes to law enforcement within three days and to file claims within a fixed period of time, usually two years. Most states can extend these time limits for good cause. If other financial resources are available, such as private insurance, compensation is paid only to the extent that the collateral resource does not cover the loss.

Crime Victims Compensation

Crime victims compensation programs in all states except Maine provide financial assistance to victims and survivors of criminal violence. Payments are made for medical expenses, including mental health counseling and care, lost wages attributed to a physical injury, and funeral expenses attributed to a death resulting from compensable crimes. Some other compensable expenses include eyeglasses or other corrective lenses, dental services, and prosthetic devices. Each state establishes its own procedures for making a crime victim compensation application, procedures to be used in processing applications, approval authority, and the dollar limits for awards for victims.

For additional information regarding the federal crime victims compensation program, contact the respective state VOCA administrator.

Compensation Procedures and Contributory
Misconduct (Ohio, for example)

The clerk of the court of claims establishes a procedure for the filing, recording, and processing of applications for an award of compensation.

The clerk of the court of claims transmits a copy of the application to a claim investigator within seven days after filing of the application.

The claim investigator, upon receipt of an application for an award of compensation from the clerk of the court of claims, investigates the claim. After completing the investigation, the claim investigator makes a written finding of fact and recommendation concerning an award of compensation. He or she files with the clerk the finding of fact and recommendation, along with all information or documents that he or she used in the investigation. The claim investigator does not file information or documents that have been the subject of a protective order. The claim investigator, while investigating the claim, may require the claimant to supplement the application for an award with further information or documentary materials, including any medical report readily available, which may lead to any relevant facts aiding in the determination of whether, and the extent to which, a claimant qualifies for an award of compensation. The claim investigator may also require law-enforcement officers and prosecuting attorneys employed by the state to provide him or her with reports, information witness statements, or other data to enable him or her to determine whether, and the extent to which, a claimant qualifies for an award. In any case where the claim investigator has reason to believe that the investigation may interfere with or jeopardize the investigation of a crime by law enforcement officers, or the prosecution of a case, he or she applies to the court of claims for an order granting leave to discontinue the investigation for a reasonable period of time in order to avoid such interference or jeopardization.

The finding of fact that is issued by the claim investigator includes:

1. Whether the criminally injurious conduct that is the basis for the application did occur, the date, and exact nature of the conduct;
2. If the criminally injurious conduct was reported to a law enforcement officer or agency, the date it was reported, the name of the person who reported it; or the reasons the conduct was not reported; and why it was not reported within 72 hours after the conduct occurred;
3. The exact nature of the injuries that the victim sustained as a result of the criminally injurious conduct;
4. If the claim investigator is recommending that an award be made, a specific itemization of the economic loss that was sustained by the victim, the claimant, or a dependent as a result of the criminally injurious conduct;
5. A specific itemization of any benefits or advantages that the victim, the claimant, or a dependent has received or is entitled to receive from any collateral source for economic loss;
6. Whether the claimant is the spouse, parent, child, brother, or sister of the offender, or is similarly related to an accomplice of the offender;

7. Any information which might be a basis for a reasonable reduction or denial of a claim because of contributory misconduct of the claimant or of the victim through whom he or she claims; and
8. Any additional information that the claim investigator deems to be relevant.

The recommendation that is issued by the claim investigator contains

1. Whether an award of compensation should be made to the claimant and the amount of the award; and
2. If the claim investigator recommends that an award not be made to the claimant and the reason for the decision.

The claim investigator files his or her finding of fact and recommendation with the clerk within six months after receiving the filing of the application.

Upon receipt of the claim investigator's report, the clerk of the court forwards a copy to the claimant with a notice informing the claimant that any response must be filed within 30 days of the date of the notice. After the expiration of such 30-day period, the clerk assigns the claim to a judge or commissioner of the court. The judge or commissioner reviews the finding of fact and recommendation, together with any response submitted by the claimant. If deemed appropriate, the judge or commissioner may request the claim investigator to comment in writing on the claimant's response. Within 45 days, the judge or commissioner evaluates the claim without a hearing and either denies or approves an award of compensation to the claimant.

Except in the case of death, compensation payable to a victim and to all other claimants sustaining economic loss because of injury may not exceed $25,000 in the aggregate. Compensation payable to all claimants because of the death of the victim may not exceed $35,000 in the aggregate.

If an award of compensation of $5,000 or more is made to a minor, a guardian shall be appointed to manage the minor's estate.

If the claimant or claim investigator disagrees with the approval or denial of an award, either can request a hearing. Such request is filed within 21 days after notification of the judge or commissioner's decision.

At a hearing a judge may cross-examine witnesses, require evidence not produced by the parties, stipulate questions to be argued by the parties, and continue the hearing to allow time to permit a more complete presentation of the claim. After the close of the hearing, the judge or commissioner shall consider the claim and conclude his or her determination within 30 days.

Disenfranchisement

There is a societal tendency to marginalize the bereaved by disenfranchising them, by isolating them from the rest of society. Doka [2] calls this isolation disenfranchisement.

In American society, it is often thought that those who are murdered have in some way brought it on themselves [3, 4]. Most people do not want to think that murder could happen to their family or their loved ones, so they tend to blame the victim. People often do this to protect their own sense of vulnerability. In projecting the blame on the victim or the survivor, people create a sense of security. By doing so they feel their family is somehow exempt from the tragedy of murder. Projecting the blame creates an internalized sense of security for the observer and emotionally distances him or her from the homicide victim. They are clearly "different" from the homicide survivor. This same sense of security and distancing occurs in other traumatic events, but the definition of murder adds the intentions of a third party. The reality of a person intentionally killing another person is a reality most people do not want to face.

> People have a problem considering that the unspeakable can happen to them. Blaming the victim in a homicide is a less disturbing alternative than facing the uncertainty of life [4, p. 12].

Society in general has a tendency to distance itself from the homicide survivor by attaching a stigma to the type of death and by disenfranchising the survivor.

Complications with grief occur when a death is socially unspeakable. There are some deaths that are perceived as not worthy or openly sanctioned by society. These are stigmatized deaths and would be classified by Goffman [5] as falling within the stigma category of "blemishes of individual character."

> While the stranger is present before us, evidence can arise of his possessing an attribute that makes him different from others in the same category of persons available for him to be, and of less desirable kind—in the extreme, a person who is quite thoroughly bad, dangerous, or weak. He is thus reduced in our minds from a whole and usual person to a tainted, discounted one. Such an attribute is a stigma, especially when its discrediting effect is very extensive. . . . It constitutes a special discrepancy between virtual and actual social identity. . . . Not all undesirable attributes are at issue, but only those which are incongruous with our stereotype of what a given type of individual should be [5, p. 3].

Spungen states, "most homicide survivors are astounded to discover that the violent death of a loved one carries with it an explicit social stigma" [4, p. 12]. In many homicide cases, the loss is socially and morally undervalued, and even devalued. In many situations, the murder victim is stigmatized, as is the family, so the loss is considered illegitimate or not worthy of grief. Michalowski's article on the social meanings of violent death states, "It is the manner of dying, not the death itself, that determines the social meaning of any death" [6, p. 83]. The social meaning or lack of meaning creates a social stigma. In cases of stigmatized death, the grief is disenfranchised.

> Disenfranchisement can occur when a society inhibits grief by establishing "grieving norms" that deny such emotions to persons deemed to have insignificant losses, insignificant relationships, or an insignificant capability to grieve [2, p. xiv].

In American society, mourners are cast into disenfranchised grief because: 1) the relationship is not recognized, the relationship is not based on traditional kin ties such as friend, co-worker, or cohabitant partner, or the relationship is not socially sanctioned such as a homosexual relationship or extramarital affair, or the loss exists in the past such as an ex-spouse or former friend; 2) the loss is not recognized or socially defined as significant such as perinatal death, abortion, or the death of a pet, or the reality of the death is not socially validated such as the loss of a person as we know them because of Alzheimer's disease; or 3) the mourner is not recognized as capable of grieving (children, the elderly, or mentally handicapped). Rando [7] adds three additional reasons for disenfranchised grief: 4) the mourner's social group does not support the loss—members are defensive and want to protect themselves, such as when the death is mutilating or the death of a child, or they want to protect themselves from embarrassment, as in a stigmatized death such as autoerotic asphyxiation; 5) support may be withheld as punishment such as after an AIDS death or criminal act; and 6) a devalued person may be viewed as not worthy of grief, such as an alcoholic or a person with a disability. The mourner's social group may recognize the loss but respond as if they do not. Victims of homicide are often devalued because of the perceived or real blame associated with the death [4].

Because of a stigmatized death, the survivor may be denied the usual means of mourning, which leads to social isolation and emotional withdrawal of the survivor [2-4]. The simultaneous availability of support and lack of support is worse than complete unavailability because it tends to increase secondary loss and intensify feelings of shame, victimization, despair, depression, search for meaning, and social withdrawal [7]. In a study of lesbian women, Deevey reports that some lesbian women who were expected to be supportive of their mourning friends often were not and that "unpredictability of support appeared more of a problem than universal lack of support" [8, p. 13]. Fowlkes reports that

> Stigmatized loss, shrouded in secrecy or shame, leaves the mourner scandalized by or destitute in grief, actually at odds with the social milieu . . . and [leads the mourner] to distrust the very legitimacy of grief itself [9, p. 651].

Rando contends that difficulties arise when a mourner's perceived need for support is not met. These difficulties are "exacerbated when the disenfranchised mourner recognizes that the support is available but is being withheld for some reason" [7, p. 499]. A lack of social support has been associated with poor bereavement outcomes as measured by poor health in the first year after the death [10-14], continued distress two years after the death, an increased use of anti-anxiety medications [15], and increased stress in adjusting to the role of widowhood and a single person [16]. The societal isolation and projection of blame on the victim often leads to victimization.

Web Sites

U.S. Department of Justice, Bureau of Justice Statistics
http:/www.ojp.usdoj.gov/bjs/homicide

U.S. Department of Justice, Office of Justice Programs
http:/www.ojp.usdoj.gov/factshts

Ohio Legislature
http:/www.legis.stste.w.v.us/Joint/Court/victims

References

1. Bureau of Justice Statistics, *Reports to the Nation on Crime and Justice,* U.S. Department of Justice, Washington, D.C., 1999.
2. K. Doka, *Disenfranchised Grief: Recognizing Hidden Sorrows,* Lexington Books, New York, 1989.
3. L. M. Redmond, *Surviving When Someone You Love was Murdered,* Psychological Consultation and Education Services, Clearwater, Florida, 1989.
4. D. Spungen, *Homicide: The Hidden Victims,* Sage, Thousand Oaks, California, 1998.
5. E. Goffman, *Stigma,* Prentice-Hall, Englewood Cliffs, New Jersey, 1963.

6. R. Michalowski, The Social Meanings of Violent Death, *Omega, 7,* pp. 83-93, 1976.
7. T. A. Rando, *Treatment of Complicated Mourning,* Research Press, Champaign, Illinois, 1993.
8. S. Deevey, Cultural Variation in Lesbian Bereavement Experiences in Ohio, *Journal of the Gay and Lesbian Medical Association, 4*:1, pp. 9-17, 2000.
9. M. R. Fowlkes, The Social Regulation of Grief, *Sociological Forum, 5,* pp. 635-652, 1990.
10. R. Glick, R. Weiss, and C. M. Parkes, *The First Year of Bereavement,* John Wiley and Sons, New York, 1974.
11. D. C. Maddison and W. L. Walker, Factors Affecting the Outcome of Conjugal Bereavement, *British Journal of Psychiatry, 113,* pp. 1057-1067, 1967.
12. D. C. Maddison, A. Viola, and W. L. Walker, Further Studies in Conjugal Bereavement, *Australian and New Zealand Journal of Psychiatry, 3,* pp. 63-66, 1969.
13. C. M. Parkes, *Bereavement and Studies of Grief in Adult Life* (2nd Edition), International Universities Press, Madison, Connecticut, 1972.
14. B. Raphael, *The Anatomy of Bereavement,* Basic Books, New York, 1983.
15. V. Mor, C. McHorney, and S. Sherwood, Secondary Morbidity among the Recently Bereaved, *American Journal of Psychiatry, 143*:2, pp. 158-163, 1986.
16. E. A. Bankoff, Peer Support for Widows: Personal and Structural Characteristics Related to its Provision, in *Stress, Social Support and Women,* S. E. Hobfill (ed.), Hemisphere, Washington, D.C., pp. 207-222, 1986.

CHAPTER EIGHT

Rita

Rita is a 50-year-old woman who is retired and on disability. Rita's children are grown and have moved on. She lives in the same house that she, her mother, and grandmother lived in for years. She lives alone in a small rural community. I met Rita at her house early one afternoon.

Rita's mother (who died 21 years ago at the age of 57) was murdered while she was at work in 1978.

"He came by the dry cleaners twice. He robbed the place. After he left Mom followed him outside and got the license plate number. She went back in the store and called the police. He came back in while she was on the phone and he shot her in the back.

"I was working at the nursing home and I got called in the office. They said they received a phone call that my mother had had an accident and she was at the hospital. The news shook me up so one of the nurses volunteered to take me to the hospital. It wasn't until I got to the hospital that I found out what happened. Well that was one shock.

"Then I had to go verify the body and I wasn't permitted in the room. I had to stand at the door. I think that was the most awful part because I guess I wanted to go over and hold her and stuff like that.

"Then they wanted to do an autopsy and my idea of an autopsy is like when you cut them up. I didn't want that but I was told they were going to do it anyway because it was a crime and they needed the bullet. I was very upset so my daughter's friend sat me down and explained an autopsy and the need for it and everything so I gave my consent. The friend was in the police department so he took pictures for me since I couldn't go in the room.

"I had the load of coming home and telling my grandmother. I had enough sense to have them call the family doctor to be there which he was and so were a couple other people. She was extremely upset. After the shock of it, her comment was, 'You don't bury your kids, they bury you.'

"Over the years my grandmother always said she just wanted to die to be with my mother.

"I didn't cry until the day of the funeral. There were a lot of people there and that helped the learning process. I learned a lot of things about my mother and father that I didn't know before then. People talked about them and it was comforting. They told stories about my mother that I had not heard before. The good things we often forget or take for granted.

"My kids went through quite a bit after my mother died. My oldest daughter got very violent at the funeral home. She went into the bathroom and was pounding her head against the wall. Her girlfriend came out and told me about it and I had to go deal with that. I feel some of the problems my kids are having now are because of that.

"I was brought up that you're not supposed to hate people but something of this magnitude. . . . It's like I've told my kids, 'I dislike people but this guy I hate.'

"The grieving process never ends. It just gets lighter and you go into a different phase of your life. You have to go on living because the deceased doesn't want you not to and you have to abide by that. I feel you make yourself more of a recluse and you pray about things that happen to you. It's still grieving but not as hard. The pain is still there. It lays dormant for a period of time then it comes out and hopefully you can control it. I think I'm to the point where I swing like a pendulum. Some things really upset me and sometimes it eases up.

"Grieving a murder is a learning experience. It's a process of growing physically and mentally. It's made me a better person.

"I had friends to talk to and stuff like that but I don't think the friends full realized everything that was going on. They were just there.

"I remember the gap in Mother's Day. I used to have all the articles that were in the papers about my mother's murder and I would go through it constantly. It started out like an everyday thing that I read the articles then it got to maybe twice a week. Then it was once month and finally to the point of maybe every three or four months.

"The support group is extremely good as far as knowledge goes. They're very kind as far as being there for you and with you. They understand. At least now I can go to a meeting and I can feel the grief for other people instead of sitting there and constantly crying like I did when I first started going to the meetings. It was terrible. Now it's not so bad.

"The police and the legal system get you to where you're a victim because they don't tell you things. I learned as I went along with the legal system. I try to pass these things on to my kids. The police pretty much kept me informed. The day of the funeral the police department was here and they said they caught the guy and he confessed but they didn't have it down in black and white or on tape and I thought 'boy are they dumb.'

"Every time the guy came up for parole, I wrote my letters to make sure he did his full time. I felt like a knight in shining armor. I was going to make sure what happened to my mother would be rectified.

"The guy got 15 years to life for murder. One day a lady called me 16 or 17 years down the line and informed me she saw the killer. He'd stopped over at his dad's house in a yellow car. She was kind of scared too because apparently he'd seen her sometime in the course of the investigation and when he pulled in the driveway he looked toward her porch. She didn't do anything, she was kind of shocked and he went in the house. That brought everything to a head again too. I don't know where the guy is at and I don't care to know just so he doesn't bother me. I don't know if I'd even recognize him.

"Dealing with the media, I'm afraid I was rude and crude. Here I had just found out my mother was murdered and they wanted all the gory details. They were calling me the day of her murder asking what happened, how did it happen and stuff like that. I got nasty and told them to call her boss if they wanted any information.

"Funeral homes are out for me. After my grandmother passed away I went through the usual mourning process for her. I would go to funerals and I would get extremely emotional. I was over at a friend's house and from there I was going to the funeral home. I cried from the time I left my friend's house until I got to the funeral home. I cried and cried and made myself very sick. The death isn't so fresh but funeral homes make it fresh for me. It's to the point where funeral homes are out for me. I tell my kids, my spirit will never be with me when I die. It will be gone. I just don't like funeral homes."

Rita also had a supportive network of friends who kept her busy. She also found the POMC support group[1] helpful because she could talk to the group members "without being judged."

Notes

Vine Program

The Vine Program. VINE stands for Victim Information and Notification Everyday. VINE's purpose is to assist crime victims and other concerned persons by providing continual access to inmate custody and

[1] POMC Web site: http://www.pomc.com

case information via the telephone. This 24-hour information hotline allows crime victims to verify the custody status of an inmate and automatically notifies registered users if the inmate has a change in custody or case status.

VINE was created in 1994 after the tragic death of Mary Bryon in Louisville, Kentucky. An ex-boyfriend murdered Mary when he was released from jail without her knowledge. A notification call from police, that was promised but not delivered, set the stage for the development of the nation's first totally automated service for keeping crime victims informed of an inmate's custody status.

VINE is a fully automated computer service that electronically links inmate custody information at the local or state prisons to the VINE call center. When new inmate custody information is sent to the VINE call center, VINE compares the inmate information to a list of users who have registered with the service. When it finds a match it immediately places calls to the appropriate registered individual(s). VINE may also monitor court information by connecting to on-site case management systems at the prosecutor or district attorney's office.

Survivors must be a registered user to be able to use the VINE program. A survivor can register any phone number in the United States, and can register to track as many offenders as he or she would like. Registration is anonymous.

VINE only monitors inmates who are in the custody of participating agencies. VINE's 24-hour customer service center's number is 1-800-865-4314. Currently VINE serves more than 650 counties across the United States.

CHAPTER NINE
Rose

Rose is an active 50-year-old woman. She is a housewife who takes care of her grandson on a regular basis. Rose has a country accent and a quiet disposition. I met Rose at her house in the country. She had a photo album for me to look at of her mother, the newspaper articles about the murder and the trail, pictures of the funeral, her mother's house, and other fond memories of her mother.

Rose's 77-year-old mother was stabbed 132 times in her own home in 1994.

"Mom was stabbed, well the newspaper said 84 times, but she actually had 132 stab wounds. When we went through the trial, they told us, the guy that did the autopsy said, that she was stabbed 132 times in two and one half minutes. It took her ten minutes to die.

"She was left in this little bathroom, the floor she had to walk on was probably 3 × 4 feet maybe a little bigger. You couldn't even get the door open because her body was lying in the bathroom. The police and fireman had to take the door off the hinges to get to her.

"It took thirteen hours to do the autopsy because every organ in her body was bruised and she had so many stab wounds. He broke into her house and he started stabbing her. He broke both her arms with a leg from the coffee table so she didn't have any type of defense. When she ran into the bathroom, that's when he stabbed her in the back and I think that was the one that went into her heart. He kept stabbing her. We had to put her in a body bag because her body would not hold the fluids.

"At 10:30 I got this weird telephone call. I answered the phone and it was the operator. She wanted to know, because I have a telephone number that is unlisted, if I would take a person to person call, she said it was one of your mother's neighbors. I started thinking, now wait a minute, this one lady that lived down the street from mom has all her sons in prison and she always came down to mom's house at 9 o'clock at night to make telephone calls. And I thought she'd talked mom into taking her to go see her sons in prison. I thought no because I'd have to pay the telephone bill so I said no I wouldn't accept it. The operator told her no she won't accept it and I heard her say something about 'something funny is going on down at your mom's' so I thought I'd better call mom's house. So I called mom.

"I called her house and a guy answered the phone. I didn't recognize the guy's voice. I thought who is this; maybe I got the wrong number. I asked if mom was there and he said 'yes but she can't come to the phone.' Then he says to me, 'who are you?' I said 'I am her daughter' and he started questioning me. I said I wanted to talk to mom and he said 'she's been hurt.'

"So I thought maybe she fell or something. But I didn't hear mom's voice in the background and mom never stopped talking. Mom's voice was going constantly. The only time she shut up was when she went to sleep. She was always talking. I never heard her voice and that worried me.

"He said, 'We're going to be taking your mother to the hospital in a little bit. We're going to take her to St Joe's. Meet us over at the hospital. I'll call you back.' In the meantime, I'm not one to sit and wait for something like that, so I called my brother but he was out. His son came home so I told him. After my brother got home, he called me and I told him what the police officer had told me. He came over and says 'let's go over to the hospital.'

"One of the ladies that lives down the street from mom called my daughter and told her mom was dead. Stone cold, 'your grandmother's dead.' She calls me and tells me mom was dead. I just couldn't grasp that. I thought someone was pulling my daughter's leg.

"We went to the hospital and we asked them at the hospital but we were told no one has come in by that name. So my brother calls over to my mom's house and he got the same police office that talked to me. He says, 'We'll be bringing your mother in shortly.' My brother says to him, 'just tell me the truth, is mom dead?' He says, 'we really don't like to tell you over the phone but yes she is dead.'

"We didn't leave the hospital, I think it was 4 or 5 in the morning. We had to wait for them to get there and then wait for the hospital staff to get mom ready so we could see her. We got to see her but they had covers clear up to her neck so we couldn't see anything. We could see one stab wound in her face but we weren't allowed to touch her or anything."

Rose's mother, "was a very poor lady. She just had what she needed to get by with. The living room suite she had she probably got back in the 70s. She kept everything she had. I think the only new thing she had in the house was her gas stove and she'd just bought that."

Rose's mother had always gone to church; in fact she was the secretary for the church. Rose's mom was the kind of person that, "would do anything for anybody I don't care who it was." She liked people. Everyone in the neighborhood knew her; everyone in the neighborhood liked her. Everyone thought she was a sweet old lady. Her death took a toll on the whole neighborhood.

"We always thought that God would always protect you from things like that, that things like that only happen to bad people. But I have come to realize that it's not the bad people that bad things come to, it's the good people because we are far more naïve of the things going on out there in the world and we don't fear because we're not taught to. If you go to church all the time, you're taught to love and to have respect for other people and other people's things. You just don't realize bad things like robbery and murder could happen to you.

"My dad passed away in July that year and the night he died he called me and he told me, 'Rose, you get your mom out of here. You don't let her stay here because a black guy is coming in to murder her.' And that's exactly what happened. It was like five o'clock in the evening that he called me and it was about a quarter past twelve that he passed away.

"Mom was killed in December. It was strange. Dad died in mom's birthday month and mom died in Dad's birthday month."

The man that killed Rose's mother was 44 years old at the time. He was given a sentence of 33 years to life, which means he is eligible for parole after 33 years.

"He'll be the same age mom was when he killed her when it's time for him to come out. If he comes out. I hope he dies. I really do. He doesn't deserve out. People tell me he'll be too old to do anything but that's baloney. You know I do have thoughts of him coming out sometime and him trying to find us to try to kill us. He also has a son that I always have feelings that maybe when he grows up that he'll be doing that same thing and that maybe he'll come after us because he blames us for his father spending time in prison."

When asked what would be helpful to homicide survivors, Rose said it "is having someone listen to your story and someone explain what the court process would be like."

Notes

Visits from the Afterlife

Some people believe that visits from the afterlife provide comfort and/or guide the living, that the visits provide an everlasting connection between the living and the dead. According to Lee Lawson's book *Visitations from the Afterlife: True Stories of Love and Healing* [1], a spontaneous encounter with a loved one who has passed on into the next world is a life altering and transformative experience. Lawson claims that sometimes a loved one returns to say "good-bye for now," or to bring a vision of the afterlife or a lesson for this life. Often the spirit brings the blessed peace of healing to the grieving one. These extraordinary moments of reunion leave the living blessed and forever changed.

According to a recent *USA Today*, CNN Gallop Poll, almost 70 million Americans believe that it is possible to communicate with the dead and millions of people the world over have experienced a visitation.

Sense of Presence

Mystical experiences are common experiences. Survivors report communications from their deceased loved ones including a vague sense of the presence of the person who died, feeling touches, hearing voices, and smelling aromas associated with the loved one [2]. Schuchter and Zisook [3] report that auditory, visual, and hallucinatory experiences are commonplace. The bereaved communicate with the deceased, feel them hovering over, watching out for them, and protecting them.

> It seems appropriate to put sense of presence in the category of one of several types of experience that are possible during grief. Sense of presence may be more likely when mortal threats are present, when communication of feelings of grief is discouraged, or when the widow [survivor] feels helpless. However, sense of presence also represents positive coping with the existential issues and transformation of the internal relationship, and as such need not be seen as a symptom of anything [4, p. 194].

Sixty percent of bereaved people report experiences of sensing the presence of the deceased. Over 85 percent found the experiences comforting [5].

Symbols

Rainbows are often associated with the deceased. Eleonore Lehr [6] says a rainbow is considered a phantom bridge, passable only by discarnate entities that links two points. The two points are a place of danger and a place of transition and transformation.

Continued Relationships

Silverman and Nickman note that

maintaining an inner representation of the deceased is normal rather than abnormal. It also is more central to survivors' experience than commonly has been recognized. We suggest that these relationships can be described as interactive, even though the other person is physically absent [7, p. 349].

Attig [8] maintains that one can have a relationship with the deceased without being pathological and that a relationship with the deceased can be healthy and life affirming. The survivor must let go of the deceased's physical presence, fervent longing for their return, and "any singular, sometimes preoccupying, focus on them and their absence" [9, p. 284]. By making room in the survivor's heart, the deceased can continue to play an active role in the survivor's life.

Linking Objects

Various mementos serve as "linking objects" that connect us to the loved one. The mementos create a sense of continuity by providing a tangible connection with the deceased. Linking objects hold multiple meanings related to death and to the deceased. Referring to the work of Volkan [10, 11], Rando suggests that

> Linking objects are tokens of triumph over the loss and that they mark a blurring of psychic boundaries between the mourner and the one mourned [12, p. 127].

Klass [13] has observed the importance of linking objects as a source of solace for the bereaved.

References

1. L. Lawson, *Visitations from the Afterlife: True Stories of Love and Healing*, Harper, San Francisco, California, 2000.
2. J. Lord, *No Time for Goodbyes: Coping with Sorrow, Anger, and Injustice after a Tragic Death*, Pathfinder, Ventura, California, 1987.
3. S. Schuchter and S. Zisook, The Course of Normal Grief, in *Handbook of Bereavement*, S. Stroebe, W. Stroebe, and R. Hansson (eds.), Cambridge University Press, New York, pp. 23-43, 1993.
4. R. D. Conant, Memories of the Death and Life of a Spouse: The Role of Images and Sense of Presence in Grief, in *Continuing Bonds*, D. Klass, P. R. Silverman, and S. L. Nickman (eds.), Taylor & Francis, Washington, D.C., pp. 179-196, 1996.
5. S. Datson and S. Marwit, Personality Constructs and Perceived Presence of Deceased Loved Ones, *Death Studies, 21*, pp. 131-146, 1997.
6. E. Lehr, Die Bruek: Symbolic und Bedentung/The Bridge: Symbolism and Meaning, *Analytische Psychologie, 25*, pp. 297-311, 1994.

7. P. R. Silverman and S. L. Nickman, Concluding Thoughts, in *Continuing Bonds*, D. Klass, P. R. Silverman, and S. L. Nickman (eds.), Taylor & Francis, Washington, D.C., pp. 349-355, 1996.

8. T. Attig, *How We Grieve: Relearning the World*, Oxford University Press, New York, 1996.

9. T. Attig, *The Heart of Grief: Death and the Search for Lasting Love*, Oxford Press, New York, 2000.

10. V. Volkan, Typical Findings in Pathological Grief, *Psychiatric Quarterly, 44*, pp. 231-250, 1970.

11. V. Volkan, The Linking Objects of Pathological Mourners, *Archives of General Psychiatry, 27*, pp. 215-221, 1972.

12. T. A. Rando, *Treatment of Complicated Mourning*, Research Press, Champaign, Illinois, 1993.

13. D. Klass, The Deceased Child in the Psychic and Social Worlds of Bereaved Parents, in *Continuing Bonds*, D. Klass, P. R. Silverman, and S. L. Nickman (eds.), Taylor & Francis, Washington, D.C., pp. 199-215, 1996.

CHAPTER TEN

Judie

"The night my husband was killed I was given Valium to calm me down. I was hysterical and in shock, so that made sense. It did seem to help; at least it numbed the pain and I was able to sleep without the terrible nightmares.

"The first couple of months I was merely going through the motions. I was in shock and all I wanted to do was sleep. I couldn't believe he was really dead. I kept waiting for him to come through the door.

"My sister stayed with me the first month so she made all the decisions. There were many decisions to be made and I wasn't ready to make any of them.

"Within two months I moved across the country to be closer to home. It was a bittersweet decision to move. I liked it where I was, as did my daughter, but the place was a constant reminder of my husband. Dan was very popular in the community, at work, and in church. We had so many friends, but after his death people quit talking to me. They didn't know how to react or what to say, so they avoided me. People were extremely uncomfortable if I talked about Dan and quickly changed the subject or avoided me altogether. The couples that we did things with were uncomfortable seeing me because it made them think about what they would do if their spouse suddenly died. That alienation had a lot to do with my decision to move. At least by being closer to home I'd have my family to support me or so I thought.

"Most of my family acted the same as everyone else, afraid to say anything so they said nothing. They did not want to talk about Dan's death because I did get upset and they thought that made things worse instead of better.

"My daughter moved in with my sister and I started a new job in a new town. I hoped things would be better by going to a place where no one knew Dan so they would not ask about him or avoid me because they knew him, but things were not better.

"Because no one was apprehended for my husband's murder, my family and I became targets of a police investigation. The police constantly harassed us overtly and covertly. The police would try to pit one family member against the other by saying one person said something about the other person. For example, they told my brother-in-law that my sister, his wife, had a boyfriend in an attempt to upset him. The police threatened my brother-in-law's medical license if he didn't make a statement against my sister and I. My brother-in-law never thought the police would be anything but helpful, but after catching the police in a couple lies, he refused to cooperate and hired a lawyer. I did the same. That pretty much ended the harassment by the police for my family.

"My ordeal however, was far from over. Besides a search of my house, garage, and car where I used to live, my new apartment was also searched. I underwent a polygraph test, finger printing, and several unpleasant interviews. My e-mail was monitored, my phones tapped, and I was followed everywhere I went. People at work noticed these activities and started acting strangely. I'd see people looking at me, pointing and whispering. They heard the rumors and it was obvious I was under investigation. Very few people talked to me and some that did when I first got there quit shortly thereafter. They did not want to be associated with a possible killer.

"The police even harassed my daughter while she was in school. Fortunately the principal put an end to that very quickly. She was only 14 years old.

"The trauma of my husband's death and resulting stress in my life lead me to see a psychologist and psychiatrist. I was prescribed tranquilizers, sleeping pills, and anti-anxiety medication. When the police investigation threatened my retirement, the stress increased and the medications were increased. I was seeing a therapist who did not understand why I was not 'getting over' my husband's death so I was diagnosed with a chronic adjustment disorder. Again the medications increased. At the time I felt I needed something to cope with the living nightmare.

"I was a zombie most of the time. I'd forget my name, where I was going, what I was doing, and how I got to where I was. I couldn't concentrate. I could barely think. I can remember getting in my car and forgetting why I was in it or where I was going. I'd remember getting off work but not the four-hour drive to my sister's house. The work environment became hostile because I wasn't functioning properly and wasn't doing my job as well as I should have been able to nor did people understand why I wasn't 'getting better.' I entered the outpatient mental health program that, if nothing else, got me away from the hostility at work.

"At one point my boss said to me, 'You're pathetic. I went through a nasty divorce that was much worse than what you're going through and I got through it so should you.' I could not believe she was comparing a divorce to a murder. She had a *choice* in a divorce; murder leaves no choices. She could still see her ex-husband; my husband was in a box on the mantle. I was devastated by her remarks and lack of understanding.

"I tried several times to retire but was denied because of 'the investigation.' My promotion benefits were withheld because of the investigation. My life was literally put on hold and traumatized because of 'the investigation.' I was being held without my consent.

"Eventually the medications became detrimental to my health. Besides being out of touch with reality most of the time, I became anorexic. I lost twenty pounds, looked gaunt and sickly. I was sick all the time with stomach problems, headaches, and flu symptoms. I was also more accident prone because I was always out of it. My brother-in-law insisted I quit the medications before I died. My friend Sarah also insisted it was necessary so I slowly quit taking the medications.

"Because I was in such a controlled environment I didn't tell my therapist I quit taking the medications. That would be considered ignoring medical advice, which is a punishable offense in the military, or so I was told.

"The therapist was convinced I had this chronic adjustment disorder and nothing but 'recovery' from my husband's death was going to change her mind.[1] Her idea of recovery was that I no longer missed my husband, that I no longer talked about him, and that I no longer cried at the thought of him. I wasn't ready for that. I loved him and I missed him.

"Eventually the police gave up their pressure tactics and I was able to retire. Four years after my husband's death the prosecutor's office admitted that so many mistakes were made during the murder investigation that the case would probably never be solved. They never apologized for the way they treated my family, they just acknowledged that mistakes were made.

"I believe that I was given medications as a way to control me and keep me quiet. I was so far out of it most of the time; I didn't care that my every move was being monitored. I didn't question the

[1] Health Center Web site: http:/www.health-center.com/meantalhealth/adjustment

ethics of the police behavior or even the therapist's behavior until I stopped the medications. I didn't understand what was happening to me until I stopped the medications, but by then it had been nearly two years.

"I also think the therapists put me on medications because they didn't know what else to do with me. I attended their widow's group and their depression group but I wasn't 'over' my husband's death. One therapist admitted she had never treated anyone whose husband had been murdered or that was the subject of a murder investigation and she did not know what to do.

"The psychiatrist, a civilian, said he had to turn his notes from our session over to the police each time we met. He said he didn't like the idea but he did not have a choice. After I found that out I was guarded in what I had to say. It wasn't safe to talk to anyone anymore. Therapy wasn't therapy; it was another police interrogation all over again.

"Each time I took a psychological test, the interpreter suggested I exaggerated my feelings because after two years I still missed my husband, still felt his presence, still cried everyday, still felt depressed and lonely because he was gone, and thought about suicide more than once. They just didn't understand homicide bereavement; they never considered post traumatic stress, or trauma of any kind for that matter.

"The mental health professionals, my boss, and those around me had preconceived notions of recovery in one year and refused to accept anything else. Unfortunately their perceptions cost me a diagnosis of chronic adjustment disorder.

"Because of the way I was treated when my husband died, I decided acceptance and tolerance was not the answer. People need to know homicide bereavement is different and that labeling someone as abnormal, or in my case with a chronic adjustment disorder, is not always the answer.

"Education is the answer and the way to understand homicide survivors and their experience of bereavement is to talk to them about it. Listen to the stories without judgment and encourage personal, emotional, and spiritual growth when the *survivor* is ready. Personal growth can be in the form of higher education, increased self-esteem, and self-confidence. Emotional growth might be encouraged as developing new relationships, perhaps with someone alienated during the grieving process or expression of emotions in safe ways. After a murder some survivors turn away from their faith and away from God. Perhaps an invitation might take them back to their place of worship."

Notes

Confidentiality

Notes from a therapist and/or physician are considered confidential and are not released without the written consent of the patient/client. Since I was in the military (and considered government property) and under investigation for conspiracy to commit murder, the military police and Office of Special Investigations (OSI) had access to my therapist's notes at any time. Since I have retired from the military, my medical records are now considered confidential and are not released to anyone without my written consent.

Chronic Adjustment Disorder

Adjustment disorders are unusual reactions to a stressful event or situation. Adjustment disorders are not the same as post traumatic stress syndrome. These reactions start within three months of the stressful event. There are many different categories of adjustment disorders, including:

- Adjustment disorder with depressed mood—people with this type of adjustment disorder often have feelings of hopelessness, sadness, or cry a lot;
- Adjustment disorder with anxiety—people usually feel nervous, worry, or experience jitteriness;
- Adjustment disorder with mixed anxiety and depressed mood—people may have feelings of hopelessness, nervousness or feel sad, worry, or cry a lot or experience jitteriness;
- Adjustment disorder with disturbance of conduct—people do not adhere to societal norms and rules—they may violate the rights of others with truancy, vandalism, reckless driving, fighting, or other endangering acts;
- Adjustment disorder with mixed disturbance of emotions and conduct—this category includes people with some emotional symptoms (e.g., anxiety or depression) and disturbance of conduct symptoms; and
- Unspecified—this category includes other reactions such as withdrawal, inhibition, and physical manifestations such as stomachaches or headaches.

Adjustment disorders are acute if they have lasted less than six months. They are considered chronic if they lasted more than six months. Unfortunately adjustment disorders are common; the exact percent of the population who experience them is unknown. Adjustment disorder can affect anyone regardless of race, age, gender, or circumstance. They depend upon personal factors that vary from person to person and over a lifetime.

PART TWO

Reactions of Grieving Loved Ones

The following chapter provides some insight as to how homicide survivors feel about their experience of homicide bereavement. Survivors from other types of death may have similar reactions or experiences as expressed by these homicide survivors. Suicide survivors, for example, have been known to have similar reactions. One homicide survivor explains the difference of homicide bereavement as,

> People who say grief is grief is grief have never faced the reality of murder. They haven't had to relive the pain each time there is an arrest or a trial or a postponement of a trial; each time there is an appeal or parole hearing; each time there is media coverage for whatever reason; or each time the survivors have to face the perpetrator when he or she or they get away with murder [released from prison, if he or she was convicted].

The reactions of the grieving survivors are clustered in themes or general expressions. The explanations that follow the themes are the homicide survivor's own words based on his or her experience and his or her reaction to the murder of his or her loved one.

CHAPTER ELEVEN

Themes from the Survivors' Stories

Homicide Bereavement is Unique to the Individual Experiencing It

"At first you're in total shock. You can't believe this is happening to you. It's something that happens to someone else, not you. It was kind of hard to deal with. Once you've been through it, you understand mostly what people are going through but you don't completely understand everything because each individual is different."

"Murder is something that is far more difficult to deal with because this is not a natural death. This is not just a violation of the person that is dead. This has stripped everybody around that person that loved or cared about that person of his or her security, his or her basic security. And it's like it goes against everything you could possible believe in. A person, who lived a decent life, lived by the rules, by society's rules, by whose ever rules and something like this [murder] happens. It just feels like it's got to be ten times worse than these people that do drugs, sleep around, and go out and do whatever. They know that they can get in trouble. They live on the edge. It's taken until not too long ago to realize, it doesn't matter what your lifestyle is. It's still the most horrible thing that can ever happen to you, to have someone you love ripped out of your life."

"The grieving process is so different from day to day. You would be having a really great time doing something fun or being with people you love or just having a good time and you'll get this wave of sadness come over you and you just can't help it. There were so many times I would just start to cry. I couldn't even say what triggered it; I would just start to cry."

"My husband and I have survived this together because we have allowed each other to grieve separately and understand each other. When it's his time to be sad and I am not sad on that particular day, I understand it and still continue to do the happy things I am doing because I can't bring him out of that sadness, and he does the same thing for me. We have learned to let each other do their own grieving."

"Everyone is different. I see victims who will be victims all their life because they refuse to be anything but. Then I see ones that you see gradually changing from a victim to a survivor, from someone who is downcast, in such a volatile state and then turn themselves around and take that volatility and turn it into something constructive."

"You continually revisit the grief issue. Every time there's a school function, a baseball game, functions with friends, whenever there's a mom and dad thing, it keeps it torn open for the kids."

"I don't think there's any set time to grieve. What you do in a week, it may take someone else a year. It may take someone else 10 years to deal with it."

"Let's just say it was a violent roller coaster ride, extremely violent. I mean from minute to minute and as time wore on, it was more like every minute to an hour to a day. It gets better, it really does. It becomes something you can live with. It isn't in the front of your mind every second."

"Everyone grieves differently. Not one person will grieve the same as the other person no matter if it's a murder or a natural death. You are going to grieve differently. You're going to have different feelings, different thoughts, different ways of coping."

"When the mortician came, he was checking her [a lady from the nursing home where Rita worked] out. He took the sheet off the top of her head and I just completely broke down. That was my way of dealing with it [her mother's murder]. I broke down completely then which was almost two months later."

"It's hard, very hard. It's not easy, nothing is easy. Until it happens to your own, that's when it hits you. Then you know. You can't do anything. You can't bring them back."

The homicide survivor describes his or her process of bereavement as: "shock," no "set time," "being stripped of your basic security," "having someone ripped out of your life," "different every day," "a violent roller coaster ride," "unique," "delayed," "very hard," and "not easy." These descriptions could also apply to other types of traumatic bereavement.

The Grieving Process Never Ends

"You never got over it. I don't expect to ever get over it. I found out, through this whole process of grieving, that it never stops. I don't think that will ever happen."

"I've done everything that I could to try to get closure but it is not possible. I know that I'm never going to forget and I don't want to forget."

"This is an ongoing thing and it goes on forever. Every time they do this [apply for clemency or early release] it's like starting all over again. That's why my life has been on hold for ten years."

"I don't think I'll ever get over it. I know I'll never get over it. Nobody will ever get over it."

"It will never heal. There will always be times when something will come up that will remind you of that [murder]."

"The grieving process never ends, it just gets lighter and you go into a different phase of your life. It's still grieving but not as hard. The pain is still there. It lays dormant for a period of time then it comes out and hopefully you can control it."

"I don't think that the grieving will ever be over. I feel the grieving is never over. I still grieve when I see certain things on TV that make me think of her and I look up at her picture and I start to cry and/or choke up. It's just a constant pain and I don't feel there's ever going to be closure as long as I'm alive myself and he's [murderer] alive. I'll never get over the loss of her; I'll never be over it."

"There's no closure, no way. There is just a new normal. A new way of coping and of living your life without your loved one."

"I don't think the grieving will ever be over," "the grieving process never ends," and "I feel the grieving is never over," are typical statements from the homicide survivors in this study based on their personal experience. Similar expressions can be found on various World Wide Web discussion groups dealing with murder and other forms of traumatic death. "Unexpected angels," for example, is one of the discussion groups.

A Homicide Survivor Experiences Positive and Negative Changes as a Result of the Murder

"I had to quit working. The doctors told me that if I didn't quit I wouldn't live another year. I needed three more years to retire with the company to get a retirement and I couldn't even stick that out. My health had deteriorated so much I couldn't work anymore."

"My social network became much larger. I have a second family with POMC. We share each other's joy and grief."

"My husband and I became very close. After this happened we became like we were when we were first married—romantic. I'd say I just needed a hug and it was like when we were young. He cuddled again. It was comforting for the both of us, he needed it too but he wouldn't say so."

"It affected me as far as my personal security. A couple days after the murder, I was terrified the killers would come here and kill us all. The terror was obvious. I still have a hard time driving in certain areas of town. I don't freak out or anything like I used to, I just know that I have to get out of there. I don't always feel safe now. I'm afraid to even have eye contact with other drivers. I watch people, anybody that comes near me. I keep my eye on them and I don't make eye contact. Even now I feel threatened by so much, in the beginning it was *everything*."

"Grief can do so many things to you and some things are good, but the majority are not good. It can motivate you. It can make you realize you still have your life ahead of you and stop wasting it. My husband, who is a habitual grumbler, it [the murder of his daughter] made him appreciate the small things in life. It made him want to go places and do things. It opened his eyes to family as being very important. He made time for the family, which is something he didn't do before."

"I gained a lot of respect for the police that I didn't have before. If my brother wouldn't have been killed, I may not have ever been to a support group for homicide survivors or gone to a courtroom and sat with families going through a murder trial. In fact, I know I wouldn't have. I'd never been in a courtroom in my life before this happened. I had no reason to."

"To me, life has always been valuable. It's more valuable now than it ever was."

"You're afraid. You never know what's going to happen. You do not know what's going to happen. You take life for granted until something like this happens because you don't think it's ever going to happen to you. You learn to be cautious."

"I have given so many speeches in school about death and dying, about the effects on the family. I've been on so many talk shows. I've been to the House of Representatives to talk about changes to the autopsy laws. I've become a spokesperson, something I never would have done before this."

"He [husband] tells me that I've changed, that I'm not the same. Well I know I'm not the same. You can't be the same after something like that happened to you. Honestly I think it's changed me for the better. I talk to more people. I don't stand back in the corner like I always used to. I usually let people know how I feel; before I never let people know how I felt. I'm more conscience of what is around me. When I'm out, I tend to look around me real good. I always make sure no one else is around me or behind me. I've done more since Mom died. I was never for the death penalty until this happened. I realize how much hurt this can cause a person and I wholeheartedly believe in the death penalty. We used to always leave our doors open and unlocked. My doors are always locked now."

"It took months before I could cook. The house was a disaster. I stayed in bed for days, not wanting to get up. I didn't care about anything or anyone, not even myself."

The negative responses to homicide bereavement in this study include the necessity to quit working because of medical complications, a developed sense of terror, avoidance behaviors, and feelings of being afraid. The traumatic nature of murder evokes fear and terror in some of the survivors and some survivors avoid those things that remind them of the deceased. The positive changes in the homicide survivors include developing a larger social network, increased closeness between family members, and a realization of what is important in life. Positive or negative, murder changes the survivors.

Most People Don't Understand the Process of Homicide Bereavement and have Unrealistic Expectations of the Survivors

"A lot of people tell you, 'You should be over it in a year.' Sometimes they'll say, 'She's been dead two or three months, you should be over it.' But there's no time limit on that. They've never been through it. My son-in-law has even told me that, 'She's gone and there's nothing we can do now. Get over it.' When family members tell you that, it's like, wait a minute, what's wrong with me? It's hard when your family members tell you to get over it. I know a lot of people think you're crazy or whatever when you go through this stuff, but it's normal. We all feel the same."

"I was let down by my church because no one came and supported me. When they see me they kind of shy away from me. They act like they are afraid to talk to me about it, but that's what we need. We need someone to talk to, someone who won't be judgmental, someone who will listen."

"People say the wrong thing or I just take it the wrong way. They don't appreciate life and they don't appreciate what I am going through. They don't understand my pain."

"Once a person is dead, it's like that's it. They don't care. That's it, like they never existed. People say to get over it but that's because they've never had it happen to them. I'm guilty of that too. Before, when Ronnie was alive, you hear about shootings and stuff. You felt bad but it never really touched you until something like this happens to you . . . I feel for every body else now, what they must be going through. I know they are hurting."

"That's what they say, 'They're dead, get on with it. He's dead, get over it. The funeral is done, he's buried, get over it.' I'm sorry but I'm not over it. It's been three years but I'm still emotional over it. When I talk about Ronnie and all that, I'm not looking for sympathy. I'm looking for understanding. People have to understand that. I don't want them to say we feel sorry for you. That isn't what I want to hear. I want you to say, 'I sorta understand what you're going through and I understand what you would like to do. I'll help you if I can.'"

"I'm supposed to forgive these people for what they did and get on with my life and maybe some day that will happen. But I'm not ready for that. They [Pope and Bishop] said I should forgive these people and go on with my life and find happiness in my forgiveness of them. Well I can forgive them, but if I do it's not going to change anything they did. It's not going to bring him [brother] back."

"I had somebody ask me, 'It's been ten years, aren't you over that yet?' I said, 'No, I'm not. It's going to take until I die. He's the only brother I had.' A lot of them [friends] didn't want anything to do with this court business or this death business. After the funeral they thought that was it, it was over, that it should be done."

"Don't ever say [at POMC], 'Maybe it was meant to be.' So many members attacked me. 'It was never meant to be. It was some asshole that murdered your daughter.' I was so floored by the whole attack I couldn't say anything back to them. 'Do any of us know God's plan? Maybe it was meant to be,' but when I said that boy were they [POMC members] irate."

"And the first people [to calling hours] had to be somebody like that, that just came to see the damages that were done to him, to see what torture looked like. I had other people during the whole time, the trials and everything; there were a few others that said very insensitive things to me. Also when the killer that was sentenced to death, before he was sentenced to death, he got a chance to say something. He got up and cried and said, 'I'm sorry, I don't want to die.' He was saying he was sorry because he didn't want to die. He wasn't saying he was sorry because he killed my son. He just didn't want to die."

"She didn't come out and say it exactly in those words but I knew what she meant and I told her, 'Betty, you don't know what I went through. You have your own grandkids. My one grandchild is out at the cemetery; I have to go out there to visit her. You don't know what I'm going through. Don't tell me I should be over it because you don't know.'"

"The thing that helps the most is being able to sit down with somebody and talk to them. Especially when a person will listen and not say, 'That's in the past and you shouldn't dwell on it.' They listen and don't interrupt. If they want to say something fine, but don't tell me I should be over it or something like that. What really aggravates me is when somebody comes up and says; 'I know how you feel. My grandmother died of a heart attack yesterday.' I say, 'You know how I felt when my mom died of a heart attack but you don't know how I feel at the loss of my granddaughter because you didn't lose a child to murder or a parent to murder. You have no idea how I feel.'"

"Nobody knew what to say. Nobody knew how to react. They didn't even try. I felt abandoned. There's just so much people don't understand."

"You should be over it in a year."

"People don't talk about him, they pretend he never existed. It's like if we don't talk about it, it never happened."

Family members, friends, and others may cause secondary victimization by their remarks such as those mentioned above. This can happen because of their concern for the survivor or from their own sense of helplessness and frustration seeing the pain and suffering the survivor must endure. And there are some people that do not understand what to do or say with any type of bereavement.

The Judicial and Other Systems Victimize the Homicide Survivor

"His [coroner] remark to me was, 'Can you bring her back to life?' I told him, 'No' and he says, 'Well you're not seeing her.' He just shut the door and walked away. I says, 'Doctor, did you do an autopsy?' 'No, I did not.' I says, 'Doc, if it is a thing of money, I will pay for it, but will you do an autopsy?' 'No I will not, by God, there is not going to be an autopsy.' And that stunned me and my wife started crying. I looked at him and said, 'Doc, what if that was your daughter?' Then he looked at my wife with a smile on his face and said, 'But its not my daughter, now I'm busy' and walked out."

"The defense tried to make my daughter look out to be a prostitute, a no good mother, a woman that ran around with every Tom, Dick, and Harry. She just lost her daughter and they were putting her on trial as if she did something wrong."

"We know what was happening now [child abuse], but they couldn't even say that this was possibly done by him in the courtroom because no one witnessed it. But if you take that and the testimony of 15 girls that he beat up while he dated them, it sure would show a pattern wouldn't it? But you can't use this in court because it had nothing to do with him murdering my granddaughter. It was in the past. It was his past behavior."

"I've been to too many trials where the prosecutors don't tell the survivors a thing; they keep them in the dark and the victim witness programs in some of these places don't help the families out at all. It's like they don't care."

"The first part [of the trial process] was finding guilt and the second part is the litigation which is the death penalty which really pisses you off because during the death penalty phase, the victim has no right to say how they feel. They have no right in court, not to make any kind of motions. While you're in court, you're told to keep quiet, and if you don't keep quiet they kick you out. You're not even supposed to cry."

"We got to see her there [hospital] but they had covers up to here [neck] so we couldn't see anything, but we could see one stab wound there [face]. We weren't allowed to touch her or anything."

"The system sucks. If the best the world has to offer is here in the United States, then the whole world is in trouble. It took two years to convict these three guys. We ended up having a mistrial the first time because there were no Black people on the jury and the defendant was Black. It was kind of like if anything could go wrong, it did."

"They had already put the remains in the coffin and once it's sealed it can't be opened again or so we were told. My mother was furious when she found out later on that that wasn't true and the coffin could have very well been opened after we got back to the funeral home."

"The detectives kept things under wraps and wouldn't tell us anything."

"We have been let down by the justice system. I told the judges, 'We have a judicial system but there's no justice.' The laws are for the criminals, not for the victim. There is nothing for the victim. The justice system is going to hell; it's just fallen apart."

"I wear a shirt that says my son was murdered so two can live the life of luxury in prison. They have it made. Free room and board, free meals, free TV, exercise, and even free schooling. What do I have? A dead son."

"When I went to verify that was her, I wasn't permitted in the room. I had to stand at the door. I think that was the most awful part because I guess I wanted to go over and hold her and stuff like that. I couldn't even get close. I couldn't say goodbye, I love you, or anything."

"The coroner had ruled her death Valium and alcohol intoxication. He did the blood test. She had .02 alcohol where she had wine for dinner the day before. Valium, she had .02 from the Valium she took the day before. For a legal dose of Valium, it would have had to be 3.5, which would have been more than 20 Valiums. He [coroner] had the blood tests that indicated otherwise yet he ruled her death Valium and alcohol intoxication. And we went through a living hell for sixteen years."

"During the trial the first day, two jurors sat in their seats and slept. One actually had his head back and was snoring. We told the prosecutor and he said he would take care of it. The next day two jurors were sleeping, the same two. A representative from the victim witness office went back and told the judge, but he did nothing."

"The prosecutor's investigator called me. 'Ray, the prosecutor wants to know if you and your wife believe in psychics.' By then we were ready to try anything. We had to meet him [psychic] in a hotel room, pay for the room, plus give him $40. Turns out [16 years later they find out] the psychic was related to the prosecutor. It was a set up."

"It's [murder case] not closed, it's just dismissed. That's the technical difference. It's like it never happened. The murderer is on the streets."

"I have seen the jury return a not guilty verdict when I knew they were guilty."

Murder is a crime against the state, not the survivor. The criminal justice system is as fallible as the people operating it are. Homicide survivors have to contend with light sentences, the crime never being solved, or the murder presented to the grand jury and not prosecuted, as well as the release of the perpetrator.

Homicide Survivors Try to Find Meaning in the Murder

"I tried to figure out why, why did he kill her, what was the purpose? I still don't understand but God told me that he killed the body but he didn't kill the soul and that's what counts."

"Every time the guy came up for parole I wrote my letters to make sure he did his full time. I felt like I was a knight in shining armor. I was going to make sure what happened to my mother would be rectified. I wanted to make sure he stayed in prison as long as possible."

"They say every thing is for a reason. Well, what's the reason for him dying? Maybe this is something I'm supposed to do? I'm supposed to move ahead and really push for legislation or get active in these groups and get something going where changes can be made. Maybe, I don't know. That's some of the things you just wonder about."

"I think support groups need to get big enough to where they have a voice in legislature. That's my intention behind everything I do. Go places to speak, that's the intention behind it, try to get a big enough group so that you can be heard. That will help change the law. You have to be heard to make changes."

"Our trial came fairly quickly so it allowed us to go on with our lives. One of the things that really allowed me to go on with my life is that I sat down and assessed everything that happened to my son and why he was here. I mean he was here for a purpose even if he only had twelve years. And I thought you [God] allowed him to be born, you made my conscience so that I could not have an abortion, that was not right for my husband and me. Then you wanted him here for a purpose. That allowed me to move on."

"I went down and fought for Victim Impact Statements in the juvenile system and it took me four years to finally get it through. That's one of my next fights, to get Megan's Law down in the juvenile area."

"I don't ask why as much as I did in the beginning. It happened, so you got to live with it. It's where I'm at now. I don't know why he [God] took one of my babies when she was only two months old but if I hadn't lost her, I don't think I would have had the strength to get through losing Stacey. Because I knew from losing my baby, that you could go on and it gets better eventually. You always hurt but you can still live your life and good things still happen to you."

"Just helping other people has helped me deal with my own grief and sorrows; being around to help them. Going to POMC meetings made me feel better and going to different trials to support families that were going through the same thing that I went through kept me going. It kept me alive."

Sometimes the Pain is Unbearable. Sometimes the Homicide Survivor Would Rather Die than Deal with the Loss of His or Her Loved One or Would Have a Desire to be with the Deceased

"Over the years, my grandmother always said she just wanted to die to be with my mother."

"I remember standing there by the coffin and the preacher saying his words, and right now I can't even remember what he said, but I had this overwhelming desire to walk to the coffin and lift the lid and go inside with him; put my arms around him and just be with him. Just shut the coffin and let me go. I can't stand this pain any more."

"I didn't even want to live. I wanted to die. If I die today I don't care because I'll be with her."

"I thought I don't care. I have this beautiful daughter and a wonderful loving husband, and a wonderful son-in-law but I don't want to live."

"I thought well if it don't work [heart cauterization], I'll be with Stacey. I just have this will to die because I don't want to go through this pain any more."

"After Ronnie's death, my father wanted to die. He wanted to end his life."

"I just didn't want to be there. I didn't want to go on living."

It's not unusual for homicide survivors to have suicidal ideation thoughts. These thoughts can be alarming if the survivor never had thoughts of dying before [1].

The Trauma of a Sudden Violent Death, Such as Murder, Often Causes Physical and Mental Consequences. Homicide Survivors Experience Physical and Mental Complications as a Result of the Death of Their Loved One

"Grandma's health started going downhill slowly but surely when my mother was killed."

"Then I realized I was actually losing my mind. I knew it but I didn't realize what I was doing to the rest of my family until my oldest daughter came in from school and said something and I yelled at her. She looked at me and stated crying and she said, 'Daddy, I wish it'd been me that died—that way you wouldn't hurt so bad.' That's when I realized that I was destroying my family, that I was losing my mind. I had to make some changes."

"Six years after the murder my health started going really bad. I was in and out of the hospital several times but I couldn't give up pursuing the killer."

"I got to the point after one year of this crying everyday that I had eye infection after eye infection from all the tears. I had to stop crying because of the physical pain. I can tell you that murder has caused so many physical illnesses in me. It's unbelievable the stress of it could do the things that it does. I was having a panic attack and it was all because of the stresses. The doctors put me on medications that I will be on for the rest of my life. All because of the stress of dealing with her murder."

"I can't stay focused and I don't remember what I am saying. The doctor says this is a stress-related thing and it could be associated with depression."

"I often say, 'The Lord will never give any more than you can handle' but I'll tell you one thing, he's got my wheel barrow running over."

"I quit taking my heart medications and when I decided that I wanted to see this guy go to jail and pay for what he did, it was too late. Not taking my medicines for high blood pressure and that, it winded up the doctors told me I needed a heart transplant. From all the stress and everything that went on, it had taken a toll on my heart. I took one pill before this happened. I take eight now every day. It's just a big difference."

"Our trial took almost three weeks and when it was over I was totally drained. Family members said I looked like I aged ten years."

"I don't remember things like I used to since Mom died. I'm not patient any more with things like I used to be. I think it's because of what I went through. When Mom was first killed, I went into a restaurant and I'd hear people complain about, 'Oh this hurts and that hurts, all this and that.' I just wanted to take and grab and shake them. 'At least you're alive, you're breathing.' I had to control myself not to do that."

"I have to read and reread and reread. I could read this page and have no clue what I just read."

Homicide survivors report affective responses including shock, cognitive responses including memory impairment and trouble with concentration, and physiological changes including cardiovascular and stress-related complications [2-5].

Homicide Survivors Experience the Pain of Losing Their Loved Ones in the Present as well as the Future

"The loss of a life is terrible but the loss of the future memories I would have had, they hurt and they hurt deep. I would love to know what she'd look like today; to see changes in her as she grows older like I did with my own kids. I feel so much was taken away from me that I'll never have with her and it will not be the same with my other grandkids."

"They stole something from me and they're stealing from me right today. Tomorrow they'll steal some more, five years from now, ten years from now, twenty years from now, if I'm still alive, they'll be stealing from me, something I could have had—my son. It's really all you have, you have memories. You have no future. There will be no grandchildren. There will be no daughter-in-law or anything like that. You'll never have it. They stole my son. They stole my future with my son away from me. It's hard to explain. You can't replace it. I never had it but I'll never have the opportunity to have it because of what they did. They stole it from me. They stole the future."

"For the three of us, it's not just the loss of her, but also of what could have been. What we are missing. We can't share our lives with her. Our granddaughter is never going to know what kind of person she [Stacey] was, what fun she was."

"If Butch were alive when my father died, instead of selling the family business, my brother would have just kept it. We wouldn't have considered selling it if he would have been alive. I'm sure my father would have loved him to take it over. My brother helped me out a lot. Now I don't have anyone to help me; instead I have to pay contractors."

"My daughter prayed fervently for six years for a new dad. She wants that father figure in her life."

"The killer robbed me of hope. Hope that things would change, that things would get better."

In addition to the loss of the individual, survivors sustain secondary losses when their loved one is murdered. Secondary losses "generate a need for grief and mourning no less than the actual death" [6, p. 410].

A Sense of Presence is Sometimes Experienced Shortly After the Death of a Loved One

"No matter what she's always there and I believe she has been back to visit me, especially one night. I went upstairs to bed by myself and I was lying there crying, thinking about her. I was saying, 'Lord I wish she was here with me.' And I'm lying on my left side and it was just like when she would be there in bed with me and she would get up on her knees and put her elbows in my side and I felt that. I felt it as plain as if she was doing it and I know she was. I jerked real quick because I thought she was there."

"There are times when I'm out at the cemetery and I am talking to her and I know she can hear me. I just know it."

"They said, 'Now we're going to have to exhume your daughter.' That was the hard part. All I could do was look at the casket. It was like she could hear me and I said, 'Baby I love you.'"

"For the first few months after Mom was killed I could hear this music. It was like heavenly music and it was far off. I could hear it but if

I said something to some one else, they'd look at me like I was crazy. For a long time, I could hear that music. As I accepted her death, it slowly went away."

"I had a dog that was diabetic and I had to give it shots everyday. One day I was filling up the needle with insulin and I happened to glance out the window and there was a big rainbow across the sky in the back yard. The most beautiful rainbow I have ever seen in my life. I was standing there by the sink and it was just like God was speaking to me, telling me everything was okay, everything was fine. And I just had this weird feeling come down over me. It was something. It was the most beautiful rainbow I've ever seen, probably six months after Mom's death. I just knew everything was alright."

"I'm not a religious Holy Roller, but I do believe in signs. The morning we went to Stacey's funeral, I stood by the casket and said I just need some sign that she was okay wherever she is. I know she's with God and I just wanted to know she was okay. After the services were over we went to the cemetery. Stacey's boyfriend's calling hours were later in the afternoon. We went to his calling hours and afterwards we went back to the cemetery because I wanted to see that her grave was covered and put together. I just wanted to see it. Chris, Mike, and I went up there. Mike and I were standing at the foot of the grave and Chris walked around to the head of the grave and she was straightening some flowers. She stood up and her mouth dropped open. Looking at the sky she says, 'My God Mom' because she heard me at the casket, and she says, 'Stacey.' We turn around and we saw the most beautiful double rainbow in the sky, a complete full arch across the sky. The one rainbow was just bright colors and the one below it was pale colors and it was like I just knew that was Stacey sending us a message that they were both okay and to my dying day I'll believe that. When my older daughter went on her honeymoon, she was terrified to go on the plane. She gets on the plane and she sees a rainbow. She just told her husband 'I can't do this and wanted to get off the plane but when she saw the rainbow, she calmed down instantly. She said, 'Stacey is on the wing. I'll be okay.' There have been other times in our lives when we have had rainbows show up. Elizabeth [granddaughter] was born January 22; there was a rainbow in the sky in the morning. That's just weird. I can't explain it but I'm glad for them. It's not just our imagination or our wish for them. They are real and other people have seen them too."

"At our house when things moved or fell for no apparent reason we'd just say 'That's Dan.' It got to be so bad [things moving/falling], the kids were freaking out. After I distributed his ashes he didn't come back as often. I guess he was finally at peace."

Some Homicide Survivors Hang on to Possessions that Remind Them of Their Loved One

"He got me a new set of pots and pans for Christmas. They were the ones with that coating on them. There's little knicks in them and stuff is coming off but I don't want to get rid of them. I know I'll never get rid of them."

"Life is not the same and it never will be because there's that empty chair, there's that room of toys upstairs, a closet with all her clothes in it that nobody will ever wear."

"I carry a stone in my pocket. That stone came from the park. It was 318 feet from the sign for the trail where they went up and shot him. That's where his body was lying in this area. I just picked up this stone and I have been carrying it ever since. It comes from the area where he was, where he last was. It's just the little things that you have."

"I remember I got that box of my brother's clothes [that his brother had been buried in for over one year before the funeral] and I put them in my car. My car smelled so bad. The inside of my car smelled so bad because it was warm outside. Even after I got home, my car still had that smell. I don't care; I'm going to smell it. It's my smell. As time went by, cobwebs started to form around this box that I put in the garage. After I moved, I took it out and put the box in my new garage. I thought it was going to do it all over again [cobwebs] but it never did. To this day I have not opened up that box and looked in the bag. I don't know what's in there. My garage doesn't smell. The box was the one thing I got that belonged to my brother. I did get that back after the trials."

"I have this box upstairs with his pictures in it that I keep for the kids."

Ron wears his son's class ring in which he has had the stone removed and replaced with a picture of his son covered with a clear stone. Mike wears his brother's college baseball jacket when he goes to memorial events or speaks publicly about his brother's death. All the homicide survivors in this study had objects that belonged to the deceased. Jack had all this granddaughter's toys and clothes. Miriam kept her son's trophies. Sue and Ray have their daughter's pictures on the walls of their homes. Amanda has her husband's pictures and mementoes in the attic and Angie keeps a poem that Corn wrote to her when he was alive. I have my husband's dog tags on my key chain.

Notes

Prison Life

There are misconceptions that people may have about prison life. It is not all luxury for the inmates. Some inmates suffer beatings, sodomy, isolation, and dehumanization. Miriam mentioned that one of her son's killers suffered from beatings from the other inmates on a regular basis. It should also be mentioned that some innocent people have been accused and sentenced for crimes they did not commit.

Secondary Victimization

The lack of response or support for the survivor at the hands of those that the survivor counted on revictimizes the survivor. The lack of support also violates the survivor's assumptive world—the assumption that the support would be available. Reactions such as isolation, blame, stigmatization, and injustice arise from others' needs to defend themselves against the fear of violence. Rando points out that such behaviors offer

> others the illusion that the death was preventable and that elements can be identified that, if avoided, will assure that such a trauma could never happen to them or their loved ones. By blaming the victim and the survivors for the murder, those attributing blame explain the event to counteract feelings of fear and anxiety arising from their own sense of vulnerability and the perception of randomness [6, pp. 547-548].

Secondary Losses

Secondary losses are a consequence of the death and the deceased's inability to participate in their lives.

> These losses can involve moving from a longtime home, giving up a set of friends, living on a reduced income, lowering of social status, no longer feeling important and needed, relinquishing dreams of the future, or no longer feeling supported and safe. The degree to which the griever is invested in any of these secondary losses will impact his or her ability to resolve the mourning process [7, p. 117].

At a more basic level, secondary losses may include the loss of a sexual partner, companion, gardener, baby-sitter, accountant, and so on, depending upon the particular role(s) performed by the deceased [8].

> Each of these secondary losses initiates its own grief and mourning reactions, which ultimately may be greater or lesser in intensity and scope than those following the precipitating loss [6, p. 21].

Myths of Mourning

Rando identifies nine common myths of mourning. These myths make the experience of bereavement "worse than it necessarily has to be" [6, p. 28] because the survivor, and those around him or her, evaluates himself or herself by the myth's incorrect information.

1. Grief and mourning decline in a steadily decreasing fashion over time.
2. All losses prompt the same type of mourning.
3. Bereaved individuals need only express their feelings in order to resolve their mourning.
4. To be healthy after the death of a loved one, the mourner must put that person out of mind.
5. Grief will affect the mourner psychologically but will not interfere in other ways.
6. Intensity and length of mourning are a testimonial to love for the deceased.
7. When one mourns a death, one mourns only the loss of that person and nothing else.
8. Losing someone to a sudden, unexpected death is the same as losing someone to an anticipated death.
9. Mourning is over in a year [6, p. 27].

References

1. D. Spungen, *Homicide: The Hidden Victims,* Sage, Thousand Oaks, California, 1998.
2. A. W. Burgess, *Rape Victims of Crisis,* Robert Brandy, Bowie, Maryland, 1984.
3. J. Gyulay, The Violence of Murder, *Issues in Comprehensive Pediatric Nursing, 12,* pp. 119-137, 1989.
4. F. Ochberg (ed.), *Post-Traumatic Therapy and Victims of Violence,* Brunner/Mazel, New York, 1988.
5. E. E. Rinear, Psychosocial Aspects of Parental Response Patterns to the Death of a Child by Homicide, *Journal of Traumatic Stress, 1,* pp. 305-322, 1988.
6. T. A. Rando, *Treatment of Complicated Mourning,* Research Press, Champaign, Illinois, 1993.
7. J. D. Canine, *The Psychological Aspects of Death and Dying,* Appleton & Lange, Stamford, Connecticut, 1996.
8. C. M. Parkes, *Bereavement: Studies of Grief in Adult Life* (2nd Edition), International Universities Press, Madison, Connecticut, 1987.

PART THREE

Summary and Suggestions for Comfort

The following chapters summarize and bring together Part One and Part Two. Murder has personal and social consequences that change the homicide survivor. The changes can cause deterioration or growth in the survivor. Since each change can lead to growth or deterioration in the survivor, the actions of that person, and those to whom he or she may turn for help, are extremely important. Each identified change is actually a possible fork in the road, a choice to be made by the survivor.

CHAPTER TWELVE

Analysis of Themes

This chapter is an analysis of the themes from Part Two and relates them to the current grief literature [1].

Major Themes Related to the Literature

Homicide bereavement affects the survivor on a personal and social level. On a personal level, the homicide survivor experiences loss, trauma, and victimization.

Personal Consequences

Loss

In addition to the loss of *the individual*, homicide survivors sustain secondary losses when his or her loved one is murdered. *Secondary losses* are a consequence of the death and the deceased's inability to participate in the survivor's lives. Secondary losses "generate a need for grief and mourning no less than the actual death" [2, p. 410].

"I don't think the grieving will ever be over," "The grieving process never ends," and "I feel the grieving is never over," are typical statements from the homicide survivors in this research. Based upon the traditional models of grief and grief work, many people believe that grief can end, that it will be over some day. However,

> research and personal experience have led this author to believe that many Americans grieving major losses will not ever reach a time when they completely stop grieving. The expectation that they can and should reach the end of their grief is based on a misunderstanding of normal grieving and does them a disservice [3, p. 45].

Most of the grief literature indicates a period of recovery or acceptance where the grieving process comes to an end, but this research indicates otherwise. Not one of the participants, some of whose loved one had been murdered as long as 21 years ago felt the bereavement process would end. It was not a matter of holding on in order to remember and not to forget, but a matter of loving the deceased and continuing that love in spite of the physical absence. Attig [4] and others grief theorists recognize it is okay and not pathological to continue a bond with the deceased.

> In their absence, the dead continue to exert an influence. No matter how bitterly we experience our loss of them, we are richer for having known them. In subtle ways, the life we shared together deepens our own ongoing life. Our experience of having known them provides us a context for further experiencing. The life that we continue to live becomes a cultured life, a life informed by instances of life lost, a life informed by death [5, p. 137].

Lord [6] refers to episodes of sadness as "grief spasms." Lord says that the bereaved experience grief spasms from time to time for years and that anniversaries are particularly difficult—the birthday of a loved one, the anniversary of the death, the wedding anniversary, Mother's Day, and Father's Day. These anniversaries come every year and evoke a response in the survivor each time. Rose says, "It will never heal. There will always be times when something will come up and remind you of that [the death of a loved one]."

The homicide survivor remembers the loved one and thinks about what could have been had his or her loved one not been murdered. Jack talks about the loss of a *future* with his granddaughter, "I'd love to know what she looked like today; to see changes in her as she grows older like I did with my kids." Ron talks about being robbed of the *future*: "There will be no grandchildren. There will be no daughter-in-law or anything like that." Sue says, "We can't share our lives with her." Mike talks about how his father's business would have stayed in the family if his brother were not murdered "I'm sure my father would have loved him to take over."

Amanda says, "The killer robbed me of hope." She refers to the hope of a better future with her husband and better life for her children that she can no longer hope for because her husband was suddenly and unexpectedly murdered. Amanda had a *basic assumption* that her husband would be there to provide for the family.

The intentional act of the perpetrator violated Rose's *assumption of safety* in the world, a sense of *personal safety and security*. Rose talked about how she now locks all the doors in her house since her mother was murdered. Rita will not go to certain parts of town without the doors locked and accelerating to the maximum speed allowed. Ron and Kim carry guns for personal protection.

Trauma

Murder is a traumatic form of death that embraces elements of dying that invoke personal terror. The death is *violent*. The participants in this study described the process of bereavement as: "shock," no "set time," "being stripped of your basic security," "having someone *ripped out of your life*," "different every day," "a violent roller coaster ride," "unique," "delayed," "very hard," and "not easy." Some of the descriptors themselves infer a sense of violence and violation indicative of homicide—e.g., stripped (torn away from), ripped (torn, uneven or rough edges), violent (very hard, and shock)—that traumatize the survivor. This is supported by Rynearson [7] who suggests that homicide is different than natural death because of the peculiarities of homicide: violence, violation, and volition. Murder is a violent act that can include *mutilation*, as was the case of Miriam's son. Murder is frequently preceded by the *violence of robbery*, which was experienced by Ron's son, Amanda's husband, and Rita and Rose's mothers. Although Rose is the only one to specifically mention a sense of violation, it is a common feeling among homicide survivors [7]. "I felt like somebody just skinned me alive" is how Rose described how she felt when she was told her mother was murdered. As an analogy, the skin serves as a protection or safety over the body. Being skinned alive just begins to describe the violation (i.e., pain and suffering) endured by homicide survivors. "Homicide is the ultimate violation that one individual can impose on another" [8, p. 162]. "Having someone ripped out of your life" is a violation, a transgressive act. Rynearson [7] describes homicide as a volition as one's own will (the perpetrator's will) to break the existing societal rule of not killing one another. A man (in this study all murderers, those causing the death, were men) deliberately chose to end the lives of the homicide survivor's loved one.

The research findings of personal trauma are similar to Rinear's [9] list of common reactions to trauma that indicate "shock," differentness everyday with "sudden waves of sadness," and the bereavement process as "not easy." The trauma overwhelms the homicide survivor, some to the point of suicide ideation. Six of the eleven participants expressed a desire to die or be reunited with their loved one. "I just didn't want to live." "I wanted to die." "I just have this desire to die because I don't want to go through this anymore." Suicide ideation is something that most people experience at some time in their life. Although it may be a fleeting thought, most people think about wanting to die or preferring to be dead when in a traumatic situation. Half of the participants made comments about wanting to die or not wanting to go on but in the context of a specific situation (as in when Miriam was burying her son or Sue was scheduled for a heart catherization) or during a short period of time. Amanda "just didn't want to be there" the first year after her husband's murder.

This study does not support the notion that death has a universal significance for the griever irrespective of the historical, cultural, familial, or personal context. Homicide is traumatic and horrific for the survivor and as such, homicide bereavement is a personal and unique process. "Grief is as individual as a person's fingerprints" [10, p. 45]. "Grief is a personal process, one that is idiosyncratic, intimate, and inextricable from our sense of who we are" [11, p. 89]. Modern theories of grief support individualism.

Homicide bereavement is not only traumatic, it is *doubly traumatic*: one not only has to cope with the loss of a loved one, but also all the issues, including stigma, surrounding the murder. This research supports the literature in that homicide bereavement is a traumatic experience. The participants in this study reported affective, cognitive, behavioral, and physiological responses associated with trauma and traumatic death. They experienced *rage, terror, numbness*, and *feelings of devastation and irritability*. They experienced *confusion, memory impairment*, and *inability to concentrate*. They experienced anxiety about their safety as well as their family's safety, avoidance of the traumatic-related stimuli and social isolation. They experienced *appetite and sleep disturbances, cardiovascular and immune system changes*, and increased *startle responses*. They experienced what has been identified as trauma. Homicide survivors experience trauma so they are not "abnormal" or "pathological" as some would label them.

Victimization

"You should be over it in a year," "They're dead, get on with it," "It's been ten years, aren't you over that yet?" "That's in the past, you shouldn't dwell on it," "You're pathetic," and "I know how you feel, my grandmother died last week" are examples of things that have been said to the homicide survivors in this study. *Family members, friends, and others* may cause secondary victimization by their insensitive and sometimes callous remarks. This can happen because of their concern for the survivor or from their own sense of helplessness. The comments can also be made because of a lack of understanding and sympathy, and/or because they do not want to face the reality that murder could happen to them. By projecting their feelings of nonacceptance, other people can somehow distance themselves from the reality that murder could actually happen to them. Oftentimes the secondary victimization is in many ways worse than the murder itself because it is at the hands of those the survivor expects to be supportive and understanding [2, 10, 12].

Remarks such as, "Aren't you over that yet?" imply that the homicide survivor's trauma and grief are a transitory phase.

> But we cannot 'get over it,' because to get over it would mean we were not changed by the experience. It would mean we did not grow by the experience. It would mean that our loved one's death made no difference in our lives [13, p. 1].

Personal Growth

Seven of the research participants indicated they experienced *positive change*(s) after the death of his or her loved one. Of the positive changes reported by the participants, Ron, Sue, and Rose talked about asking why their loved ones were killed and how that *changed their outlook on life*. Rose consoled herself by saying, "He [perpetrator] killed the body not the soul and that's what counts." For Rose, the soul is what matters after death. The body no longer has meaning. Miriam and Mike developed a second family within POMC. POMC became a big part of their lives because the POMC members were there to listen and comfort them when they needed to be listened to or comforted, unlike the rest of general society. Sue and her husband "became very close" and her husband realized the importance of family. Sue indicated her husband was always too busy to do things as a family before their daughter Stacey was murdered. After Stacey's death, Sue's husband made time, took time off work to be with his family and "he cuddled again." Rita reported teaching others what she knows and keeping her kids informed. Rita said she wanted to be sure her children knew her intentions and learned from her so that her children would not experience the confusion and uncertainty that she did when her mother was murdered. Sue is "waiting around to discover a reason" for her daughter's death because she believes "God has a reason for everything." Rita became involved in POMC and helping others through her experience of losing her mother. She also wrote all the necessary letters when appropriate to ensure her mother's killer did his full time in jail. Without the impact statements and parole denial petitions, some perpetrators are released from prison in minimum time. Jack started a POMC group in his area to help other parents of murdered children and other homicide survivors understand the nature and consequences of homicide. Jack said that by helping others he was able to find *meaning in life, meaning that keeps him alive.*

Personal understanding and meaning is important in the process of grief [14-16]. Besides looking for an explanation of why our loved one was murdered, we ask ourselves, "Who are we now?" "What's my purpose?" Until we come to terms with the murder and understand who we are as a result of it, I believe we (homicide survivors) remain victims. When we can engage in a process similar to Mead's [17] *self-reflexivity,* where we come to understand ourselves separate from and irrespective of others, we move from being a victim to a survivor.

By reflecting on self, the survivor can construct a personal meaning or *understanding* of self, which I believe moves the homicide survivor forward in the bereavement process. This forward movement allows for personal and social growth rather than deterioration. All the participants in this study were engaged in or had found new meaning in their lives. In spite of a weak heart, Jack continuously and actively supports homicide victims throughout the tri-state (Ohio, Pennsylvania, and West Virginia) area. Miriam, whose son suffered a brutal death, became a Victim Witness Program Coordinator where she helps other victims understand the court system and the grieving process everyday. Sue, Rita, Rose, and Amanda support Parents of Murdered Children (POMC) and its functions regularly. Ray and Mike have been on talk shows trying to get others to understand the consequences of murder for the survivors left behind. Ron, Jean, and Kim proudly wear buttons and T-shirts that say "my son was murdered so two men could live the life of luxury in prison" so others will realize the injustice of murder and the criminal justice system and work toward changes.

After they (the participants) decided to ignore others around them (i.e., you're "crazy" or "abnormal"), and came to *understand who they were* and what was important to them, they were able to begin to live with their grief (as a survivor) in a way that they found meaning in their lives. They were then able to move on and not give up and die. Victor Frankl [18] talks about finding meaning in life by transforming an unavoidable tragedy into a personal triumph. The personal triumph in this study relates to helping others, for example, by starting a support group, attending trials with other homicide survivors, talking to schools and the media about death, dying, and murder, and going back to school.

> Suffering leads to insight, to knowledge about what it really means to be [19, p. 54].

Prend [20] describes reinvestment as a broad term to describe the phenomenon of connecting to life again, of caring enough to dedicate oneself to the living and the future. She says you reinvest by accepting the loss and channeling your pain, creating something new or meaningful. All participants in this research project reinvested in one cause or another. Most became involved in helping other homicide survivors either through the criminal justice system or just being there to listen to them when the survivors needed to talk or be heard. "One outstanding characteristic of bereaved people is that they generally become more compassionate to others who are suffering a loss of any kind" [21, p. 9]. "If the victimization can be viewed as serving a purpose, the victim will be able to reestablish a belief in an orderly, comprehensible world" [22, pp. 25-26]. Unfortunately, "you take life for granted until something like this [murder] happens" is how Kim explained finding meaning in life.

Personal Deterioration

Four of the thirteen responses of change indicated negative change(s). Jack had to quit working because of *medical complications due to the stress* and trauma of his granddaughter's murder and the subsequent trial, "The doctors told me that if I didn't quit [working] I wouldn't live another year." Sue developed *a sense of terror, of being afraid "of everything,"* "I was terrified that the killers would come kill us." Ron reported *avoidance behaviors* such as avoiding the room where his son spent most of his time and Kim reports being afraid of "not knowing what will happen next."

The traumatic nature of homicide evokes fear and terror in the survivors, which is not found after a "normal" or natural death. Some survivors avoid those things that remind them of the deceased such as the area where the loved one was killed, the hospital where the body was identified, the funeral home, and/or the house where the victim was murdered.

The *health* of Rita's grandmother *declined* after the death of Rita's mother. Rita's grandmother had great difficulty accepting the fact her daughter died before she did. "We're not supposed to outlive our children and our grandchildren," was also echoed by Jack when his granddaughter was murdered. Ray was sure he was *losing his mind* after his daughter Sharon was killed. He felt he had to visit the cemetery everyday in order to keep going on with life. Sue experienced *chronic eye infections*, an inability to stay focused, *panic attacks*, and other *physical illnesses* due to the stress and trauma associated with homicide. Jack now needs a heart transplant and "family members said I looked like I aged ten years" after the trial. Rose and Amanda mentioned having memory problems after their loved ones were murdered. They reported *forgetting* what they were saying in the middle of a sentence, forgetting where they were going, and what they were doing. Miriam said she remembers forgetting how to make coffee when she had made coffee everyday for many years. The trauma of murder interferes with the brain's normal functioning ability for much more than the "expected" year it takes to "get over" the murder of a loved one.

Miriam is the only one to mention a sense of *helplessness*, although parents whose children have been murdered frequently experience a sense of helplessness. "It's a horrible feeling to know that your child is out there being tortured and you're not out there to help them in anyway."

Sue is the only one to talk about *regrets*. "The one thing I regret . . . I wish I'd have said 'I love you' that day." Brabant calls these regrets "if onlys."

> When death is sudden and unexpected, we are left with all the "if onlys." If only I had told him I loved him, if only I had told her I was sorry for something I did or did not do. If only, if only, if only [23, p. 39].

The participants reported affective responses including shock, cognitive responses including memory impairment and trouble with concentration, and physiological changes including cardiovascular and stress-related complications consistent with the homicide and post traumatic stress literature [8, 24-26]. The participants did not appear "pathological"; rather they appear to be coping with the horrific nature of the murder of their loved ones.

Social Consequences

Loss

Homicide results in a loss for society, a loss that is often overlooked or trivialized. Society loses an *individual*. A few years prior to his death, Amanda's husband was a pastor of a church. Rose's mother was very active in her church and served as the church's secretary. Rita's mother was an active member in the local community. Even at 12 years old, Miriam's son was active in the Boys Scouts of America and helping others. Sharon was trying to bring her addicted friends into the church and away from their addictions. Ronnie was involved in a youth soccer team. Dan was a lay minister in his church and he was involved in numerous community projects helping underprivileged families cele-brate the holidays. All the victims could have had contributions to make to society sometime in the future. As a contribution to society, nine of eleven victims were tax-paying citizens.

Most people assume that if they lead a good "Christian" life, treat others with dignity and respect, and avoid trouble they will some how be protected by society. However, murder can happen to anyone any time. Murder *shatters the assumption* that we live in a society that is reasonably safe and that if we are harmed the perpetrator will be punished. Some killers are not punished.

Victimization

Ray's story is an excellent example of victimization by various social systems. Contrary to blood tests indicating otherwise, the coroner ruled Ray's daughter's death Valium and alcohol intoxication. Despite repeated pleas to the Sheriff's department and prosecutor's office, it took 16 years before the murder was investigated. The prosecutor's office sent a man, posing as a psychic, to Ray and his family to convince them to give up on the case. The victim witness advocate and the judge congratulated the perpetrator after the jury returned a not guilty verdict. Other examples of victimization include: the defense attorney trying to make Jack's daughter look like a "prostitute, no good mother, a woman that ran around with every Tom, Dick, and Harry," and the coroner not allowing Rita to view her mother's body, "I had to stand at the door." Mike's family was also denied access to Butch's body. Not only did the coroner deny access, the funeral director told Mike's family the casket was sealed and could not be opened when in fact that was not the case. These particular actions were not attempts to spare the survivors additional pain but instead were actions to protect the systems involved. The *media* victimized Sue and Rita by asking for the "gory details" the day after their loved ones were murdered. The media victimizes society with the *sensationalism* of murder cases. The constant coverage overwhelms even the most patient people.

Murder is a crime against the state, not the survivor, and as such it is an impersonal and dehumanizing process. The criminal justice system is as fallible as the people operating in it. Mistakes are made throughout the judicial process leaving the homicide survivors to contend with light sentences, the possibility that the crime may never be solved, the murder presented to the grand jury and not prosecuted, and the release or early parole of the perpetrator. All these things add to the trauma of murder and the grief process.

> For those extenuating circumstances (i.e., a homicide with all the ensuing investigations and court appearances), grief is like a hurricane. There are periods of intense pain, followed by a period of

relative calm until the back side of the hurricane [new court appearances, a newspaper article, a pardon board hearing] hits with a gale force more severe than the previous winds [23, p. 112].

Social Growth

Ron found new meaning in his life by getting involved in pushing for *legislative* changes. He's pushing for more rights for the homicide survivor. Ron believes the prison system is too "luxurious" for the inmates and that is why many commit crimes—"they have a place to stay, three hot meals, TV, and a free education." Life in prison is for some better than life on the streets. Miriam worked four years on legislative changes such as getting Victim Impact Statements in the juvenile court system which were not permitted before her son's murder. She became a Victim Witness Coordinator so that she could assist homicide survivors through the difficult and often overwhelming court process. Ray became a *spokesperson* for changes in the law regarding autopsy procedures. Jack and Ron started POMC *support groups* to support the homicide survivors in their communities.

Rita, Jack, and Rose talked about hating the perpetrators for what they did to their loved ones. Sue and Ron mentioned thoughts of wanting to kill the perpetrators, "I dislike people but I hate this guy," and "The only thing that stopped me from killing him was my family. My friends would have helped [kill him] too." Homicide is the result of the conscious act of the perpetrator. The perpetrator decided to end the life of the loved one. It is normal for the homicide survivor to experience intense rage and murderous impulses [2, 12]. In this study, the research participants turned their rage into productive energy. The homicide survivors became social change agents rather than deteriorate to the level of the perpetrator(s).

Social Deterioration

Jack mentioned, "You want to be able to function with other people so you do what you think they want. You act the way society expects you to act so you can function with others. You *put on a front* to survive." Murder has a stigma attached to it that causes many people to avoid the homicide survivor rather than face the reality of death. To be able to interact with other people, the homicide survivor must become someone else or put on a front. They learn to hide the pain. The homicide survivor must act in an "acceptable" manner. Signs of grieving after one year are not acceptable in most areas of the United States. Amanda mentioned having social support for a couple days then "I felt abandoned." People stopped coming by and stopped talking to her. Because they were uncomfortable and they did not know what to say, they avoided her. Rather than making other people uncomfortable by the expression of his pain, Jack puts "on a show."

Amanda also expressed her disbelief that the *murder of her husband was not considered a crime.* "In my mind, there was never an issue about it being a crime." She talked about how she had been denied victim compensation because her husband's death was considered "contributory misconduct in the eyes of the law." The murder of Amanda's husband was not considered a loss because her husband supposedly "contributed" to his death by having cocaine in his possession. His death was dehumanized by society. This relates to Doka's [27] concept of disenfranchisement. Some types of deaths disenfranchise the griever from society because society does not feel the person's life had value. Drug users are not valued by American society. Angie's criminal friends were not considered worthy of grief or mourning because "everyone knows you die young living that life style."

Victimization was a central issue to this study. All the participants expressed dissatisfaction and victimization, at some level, with the criminal justice system. All participants experienced, or knew of an *injustice,* or *perceived injustice,* as a result of the criminal justice system. Redmond [10] and Spungen [12] talk about the criminal justice system and the problem it creates for survivors. It is a system that is totally foreign to most people. Even the language is different. "I'd never even been in a courthouse until this happened," "I'm surprised at how little people know about the judicial system," and "I didn't even know what a prosecutor was." The system intimidates and frustrates the homicide survivor. Education about the criminal justice process can reduce the intimidation and frustration.

References

1. Y. S. Lincoln and E. G. Guba, *Naturalistic Inquiry,* Sage, Newbury Park, California, 1985.
2. T. A. Rando, *Treatment of Complicated Mourning,* Research Press, Champaign, Illinois, 1993.
3. P. C. Rosenblatt, Grief That Does Not End, in *Continuing Bonds,* D. Klass, P. R. Silverman, and S. L. Nickman (eds.), Taylor & Francis, Washington, D.C., pp. 45-58, 1996.
4. T. Attig, *How We Grieve: Relearning the World,* Oxford University Press, New York, 1996.
5. G. Mogenson, *Greeting the Angels: An Imaginal View of the Mourning Process,* Baywood, Amityville, New York, 1992.
6. J. Lord, *No Time for Goodbyes: Coping with Sorrow, Anger, and Injustice after a Tragic Death,* Pathfinder, Ventura, California, 1987.

7. E. Rynearson, Psychotherapy of Bereavement after Homicide, *Journal of Psychotherapy Practice and Research, 3*:4, pp. 341-347, 1994.
8. V. M. Sprang, J. S. McNeil, and R. J. Wright, Psychological Changes After the Murder of a Significant Other, *Social Casework, 4*, pp. 159-164, 1989.
9. E. E. Rinear, Psychosocial Aspects of Parental Response Patterns to the Death of a Child by Homicide, *Journal of Traumatic Stress, 1*, pp. 305-322, 1988.
10. L. M. Redmond, *Surviving When Someone You Love was Murdered*, Psychological Consultation and Education Services, Clearwater, Florida, 1989.
11. R. A. Neimeyer, *Lessons of Loss*, The McGraw-Hill Companies, New York, 1998.
12. D. Spungen, *Homicide: The Hidden Victims*, Sage, Thousand Oaks, California, 1998.
13. D. Klass, *Reflections on Time and Change Healing, Grieving, Growing*, Compassionate Friends, Oak Brook, Illinois, 1983.
14. J. Bowlby, *Attachment and Loss—Loss: Sadness and Depression* (Vol. 3), Basic Books, New York, 1980.
15. C. M. Parkes and R. S. Weiss, *Recovery from Bereavement*, Basic Books, New York, 1983.
16. B. Raphael, *The Anatomy of Bereavement*, Basic Books, New York, 1983.
17. G. H. Mead, *Mind, Self, and Society*, Chicago University Press, Chicago, 1934.
18. V. Frankl, *Man's Search for Meaning*, Touchstone Books, New York, 1962.
19. R. Koestenbaum, *Is There an Answer to Death?* Prentice Hall, Englewood Cliffs, New Jersey, 1976.
20. A. D. Prend, *Transcending Loss*, Berkley Books, New York, 1997.
21. C. Sanders, *Grief: The Mourning After*, John Wiley & Sons, New York, 1989.
22. R. Janoff-Bulman, The Aftermath of Victimization: Rebuilding Shattered Assumptions, in *Trauma and Its Wake: U.S. Traumatic Stress Theory, Research, and Intervention*, Brunner/Mazel, New York, pp. 15-35, 1985.
23. S. Brabant, *Mending the Torn Fabric*, Baywood, Amityville, New York, 1996.
24. A. W. Burgess, *Rape Victims of Crisis*, Robert Brandy, Bowie, Maryland, 1984.
25. J. Gyulay, The Violence of Murder, *Issues in Comprehensive Pediatric Nursing, 12*, pp. 119-137, 1989.
26. F. Ochberg (ed.), *Post-Traumatic Therapy and Victims of Violence*, Brunner/Mazel, New York, 1988.
27. K. Doka (ed.), *Disenfranchised Grief: Recognizing Hidden Sorrow*, Lexington, Lexington, Massachusetts, 1989.

CHAPTER THIRTEEN

Summary and Helpful Suggestions

The Process of Homicide Bereavement

This research shows homicide bereavement to be a personal idiosyncratic process and that the personal reality of a loss is different for each individual. Our reaction to death is as unique as who we are. For example, my identical twin sister was with me when my husband was murdered and I have subsequently been living with her. We are closer than any two people could ever be; yet we grieve very differently. Even within the same family, people grieve differently. Ron, Jean, and Kim said they grieved differently. Ron was angry and more vocal. Jean was emotional, reserved, and withdrawn. Kim was impatient and irritable. Husbands and wives mentioned grieving differently than their spouses in this study. Jack said his wife did not talk about Lisa's death but he talked to whoever would listen. Miriam said she and her husband respected the others' way of coping. Angie turned to alcohol and drugs. The 13 people that participated in this study grieved differently. Our personality, relationship with the deceased, physical and mental health, stress coping abilities, and support system(s) factor into how we deal with the horrific circumstances murder forces upon us.

Many theories of grief emphasize a swift and efficient return to a "normal" function—to life as it was before the murder. In this study the process of grief is clearly an ongoing process that involves a permanent transformation in the homicide survivors. Rose's husband mentioned how Rose had changed. She said she was a better person because of the changes she made after her mother was killed. Amanda became the father and the mother to her four children. She went back to school and became a social worker.

The length of time since the murder varied enormously, from twenty-one years to four years, yet, without exception, the participants were very emotional in telling their story. Each participant discussed the victim and his or her relationship with the victim as well as the details of the murder. The participants discussed and displayed the way in which feelings can come over them with little or no provocation. Sue had to stop talking several times during our meeting to regain her composure. Rita also had to stop twice to regain her composure. Everyone interviewed cried or had tears in his or her eyes during the interview. "The responses evoked by the event [murder] continue long after the trauma is over—in many cases, forever" [1, p. 23].

The length of time since the murder seemed to have little difference in the emotional response of the participant as he or she was telling his or her story. Where time seemed to make a difference, however, was in the physical and mental changes experienced by the participants—perhaps because of the decrease in the level of stress over time. The emotional stress of preparing for a trial or trials, the media, family, co-workers, and friends is very taxing. The anticipation of "reliving" the murder of the loved one over several days or weeks or even months through the court system is very stressful. Jack mentioned how his family said he looked as though he aged ten years during the three weeks of his granddaughter's trial. Sue mentioned a mistrial, a second trial, and the medications she would have to take the rest of her life after her daughter's death. Coping with others and their lack of under-standing of homicide bereavement compounds the stress and anxiety. The incident of the two ladies going to see what torture looked like increased Miriam's stress and anxiety at the funeral home where her son was.

The level of commitment to social change did not seem to be time dependent. Jack and Miriam started a homicide support group in their areas within five years of their loved one's murder. Ron's son was killed four years ago and he is in the process of starting a homicide support group in his area.

The length of time since the murder may have made it easier for some to talk about the murder, as with Ray and Miriam whose loved ones were murdered 14 or more years ago, but the length of time did not take the pain away as evidenced by the tears during the interview process.

The participants in this study did not return to "normal" after their loved one's murder. They changed. The death of a loved one results in change.

> Bereaved persons often ask me if I think they are going crazy. In a real sense a bereaved person is crazy. Sanity is dependent upon living in an ordered world. When you have lost someone very important to you, there is no order in your world. There is only chaos [2, p. 28].

The deceased also leaves a void in the lives of those left behind. In some cases, the void has to be filled by those left behind. Rita became the primary care taker for her grandmother after her mother died. Amanda became the father and the mother to her four children.

In addition to role changes, the participants in this study experienced physical and mental changes as a result of the murder. The trauma literature generally associates the physical and mental changes of homicide survivors with post traumatic stress and post traumatic stress disorder. Although Sue, Jean, Kim, Ron, and I mentioned seeing a therapist, no one was treated for post traumatic stress. Four of the participants were treated for depression.

Homicide grievers are misunderstood grievers. Without actually experiencing homicide bereavement, most people do not understand its intensity. For example, Sprang, McNeil, and Wright discuss the way in which society does not comprehend the length of time needed to deal with traumatic loss, "and lack of knowledge regarding how to respond" [3, p. 162].

> When victims [homicide survivors] are not accused of creating their own pain, they are often accused of exaggerating their sufferings for purposes of compensation, or sympathy, or as an excuse to avoid responsibility [4, p. 25].

All the participants talked about the lack of understanding and insensitivity of others, even family members.

Homicide survivors are often blamed for their loss, ignored, and isolated rather than supported by significant others [5].

> Even though most trauma survivors are not formally exiled from society, they can feel like outcasts, banished from "normal" human society [4, p. 23].

Jack mentioned that sometimes homicide survivors have to act differently to be able to function in society because people "don't understand," "they don't care" as Jean said, or "they don't want to hear it any more" as Kim indicated. If survivors choose not to act differently or hide their grief, they are often not accepted and become isolated by society.

The homicide survivor's personal loss becomes a social loss. The horrific circumstances and stigma of murder generally put people off (or "stops them in their tracks" as a reviewer of my dissertation remarked), so rather than deal with the reality of murder, people avoid or ignore it—until it happens to them. Jean mentioned that she was not sensitive to other homicide survivors until her son was murdered. Now she understands the survivors are hurting.

> The ordinary response to atrocities is to banish them from con-
> sciousness. Certain violations of the social compact are too terrible
> to utter aloud: this is the meaning of the word unspeakable [6, p. 1].

Yet it is the remembering and the telling of these horrific events
that allows for the restoration of the social order and the healing of the
individual victims [6]. Homicide survivors are not easily accessible
people. The stigma of the loss, trauma, and victimization they endure
often makes them unapproachable to "outsiders." Consequently homicide survivors are often misunderstood and lonely grievers.

This book is an attempt to give voice to homicide survivors so that
they can be heard, so that they and society can begin to heal. Someone is
murdered every 22 seconds in the United States. We can no longer
afford to ignore, label, and isolate homicide survivors. There are so
many of us.

Helpful Suggestions to Comfort
Homicide Survivors and Those Who Mourn
the Death of a Loved One

When asked what would be helpful when dealing with homicide
bereavement, the survivors mentioned in this book made the following suggestions:

1. Talk to the survivor. While it may be true that the survivor might
   become emotional while discussing the loved one, it helps to discuss him or her. It is helpful to know that someone cares enough to
   ask about the deceased. This assures the homicide survivor that
   the loved one is not forgotten and that his or her life had value.
2. Listen without being judgmental. The survivor needs to express
   himself or herself without fear of being judged. Try to understand
   that the survivor may need to tell his or her story. Perhaps more
   than once. Having someone listen empathetically provides comfort
   to most grieving individuals.
3. Encourage self expression. Suggestions such as keeping a journal,
   writing letters to the deceased to address unfinished business,
   painting, dance, music, biographies, etc., are mediums that allow
   the survivor an opportunity to express himself or herself. The
   mediums provide an outlet for emotions that may not be able to be
   expressed otherwise.
4. Find a local support group and encourage attendance. Support
   groups provide instrumental, emotional, and validational support
   to the griever. Instrumental support is provided by helping with
   funeral arrangements, advising on financial matters, and helping

with personal tasks (e.g., providing meals, running errands, baby-sitting, etc.). Emotional support comes from empathetic listening. Validational support involves normalizing the grief. The survivors are not "going crazy" and most feelings and thoughts have been felt by others. It helps to know others have experienced something similar and will support the survivor through the difficult times. Twelve of the 13 homicide survivors mentioned in this book attended a Parents of Murdered Children (POMC) and Other Homicide Survivors support group. All 12 said the support group helped them in some way, either by assisting the survivor during the murder trial(s) or by sharing his or her experience with others who had a similar experience. Some survivor's indicated that by merely telling his or her story in a safe environment, he or she felt comforted and understood.

5. Encourage the survivor to see a physician. Stress can have negative physical consequences that can be treated, perhaps even prevented. Depression can also be treated.

6. Education can help everyone. Sometimes people say things that are hurtful because they do not understand the pain of the homicide survivor. There are many bereavement books and pamphlets available today that offer caring ways to relate to those in mourning. This book, and others like it, are written to help the homicide survivors understand and cope with the trauma forced upon them. Several references have been made throughout this book and additional readings are listed after Appendix C. Support networks are listed in Appendix B and various legal terms have been listed in Appendix C.

7. Encourage the survivor to stay active. Stagnation can increase a sense of isolation, despair, and hopelessness.

8. Stay in touch. Homicide survivors and murder are not contagious.

References

1. D. Spungen, *Homicide: The Hidden Victims,* Sage, Thousand Oaks, California, 1998.
2. S. Brabant, *Mending the Torn Fabric,* Baywood, Amityville, New York, 1996.
3. V. M. Sprang, J. S. McNeil, and J. R. Wright, Psychological Changes After the Murder of a Significant Other, *Social Casework, 4,* pp. 159-164, 1989.
4. A. Matsakis, *Trust after Trauma,* New Harbor Publications, Oakland, California, 1998.
5. R. Janoff-Bulman, The Aftermath of Victimization: Rebuilding Shattered Assumptions, in *Trauma and Its Wake: U.S. Traumatic Stress Theory, Research, and Intervention,* C. Figley (ed.), Brunner/Mazel, New York, pp. 15-35, 1985.
6. J. L. Herman, *Trauma and Recovery,* Basic Books, New York, 1992.

Famous 19th Century Letter Written by an Anonymous English Clergyman

"To my beloved family and friends, death is nothing at all. I've only slipped away into the next room. I am I and you are you. Whatever we were to each other that we still are. Call me by my old familiar name. Speak to me in the easy way which you always used to. Put no difference into your tone. Wear no false air of solemnity or sorrow; laugh as we always laughed at the little jokes we enjoyed together. Play, smile, think of me, pray for me. Let my name be ever the household word that it ever was. Let it be spoken without effect, without a ghost of a shadow on it. Life means all that it ever was. It is the same as ever. There is absolutely unbroken continuity. Why should I be out of mind because I am out of sight? I am but waiting for you an interval, somewhere very near, just around the corner. All is well."

Support Networks

AARP Widowed Persons Service
601 E. Street NW
Washington DC 20049
1-800-424-3410
http://www.aarp.org/grief programs
http://www.griefandloss@aarp.org

American Association of Suicidology
2459 South Ash Street
Denver, CO 80222
(303) 692-0985
http://www.suicidology.org

American Self-Help Clearinghouse
St. Claires-Riverside Medical Center
25 Pocono Road
Denville, NJ 07834
(201) 625-7101

Association for Death Education & Counseling
638 Prospect Avenue
Hartford, CT 06105-4250
(860) 586-7503
http://www.adec.org

Center for Loss and Life Transition
3725 Broken Bow Road
Fort Collins, CO 80526
(970) 226-6050
Http://www.centerforloss.com/aboutthecenter

Center for Sibling Loss
The Southern School
1456 West Montrose
Chicago, IL 60613
(312) 769-0185

Compassionate Friends National Office
900 Jorie Boulevard
Oak Brook, IL 60522
1-877-969-0010
http://www.compassionatefriends.org

Concerns for Police Survivors
P.O. Box 3199
S. Highway 5
Camdenton, MO 65020
(573) 346-4911
http://www.nationalcops.org

Hospice Association of America
228 Seventh Street SE
Washington, DC 20003
(202) 546-4759
http://www.nahc.org

Mothers Against Drunk Driving (MADD)
511 East John Carpenter Freeway, Suite 100
Irving, TX 75062
1-800-438-MADD
http://www.madd.org

The Dougy Center
The National Center for Grieving Children and Families
P.O. Box 86852
Portland, OR 97286
http://www.dougy.org

Tragedy Assistance Program for Survivors
2001 S Street NW #300
Washington, D.C. 20009
1-800-959-TAPS
Http://www.taps.org

Pen-Parents
P.O. Box 8738
Reno, NV 89506
1-702-322-4773
http://www.penparents.org

Homicide Survivors
A Circle of Friends
Columbus, OH
(614) 275-4587
Email: XhomicideX@aol.com

National Organization for Victims Assistance
1757 Park Road NW
Washington, DC 20003
1-800-879-6682 (information and referral)
(202) 232-6682 (counseling line)
http://www.icfs.org

National Hospice Organization
Suite 901
1900 North Moore Street
Arlington, VA 22209
(703) 243-5900

Parents of Murdered Children
100 East Eighth Street
Cincinnati, OH 45202
1-888-818-pomc
http://www.pomc.com

Web Sites

Adult Sibling Grief
On line support for adult siblings
http://www.adultsiblinggrief.com

GRIEFNET
On line grief support
Http://www.griefnet.com

GROWW
Online support for sudden losses
http://www.groww.com

Murder Victims
http://www.murdervictims.com

WidowNet
Online self-help and information resource for widows and widowers
http://www.fortnet.org/widownet/

Victim Issues

U.S. Department of Justice
Office of Justice Programs
Office for Victims of Crime
Washington, D.C. 20531
http://www.ojp.usdoj.gov/ovc/

National Center for Victims of Crimes Victim Services
1-800-FYI-CALL
http://www.ncvc.org

National Coalition of Homicide Survivors, Inc.
C/o Pima County Attorney
32N Stone, 11th Floor
Tucson, AZ 85701
(526) 881-1794
http://www.mivictims.org/nchs/

Legislative Issues

Citizens Against Homicide
P.O. Box 2115
San Anselmo, CA 94979

Justice for Murder Victims
P.O. Box 11670
San Francisco, CA 94116-6670
(415) 731-9880
    Assists victims working with the justice system
http://www.vocal-jmv.org

Other

Bereavement: A Magazine of Hope and Healing
Bereavement Publishing, Inc.
5125 North Union Blvd, Suite 4
Colorado Springs, CO 80918
1-888-604-4673
http://www.bereavementmag.com

Legal Terms

Terminology used in the criminal justice system can be intimidating and overwhelming for the homicide survivor. Below is a list of commonly used terms that may prove useful.

1983 lawsuits—Civil suits brought under Title 42, Section 1983 of the United States Code, against anyone denying others of their constitutional rights to life, liberty, or property without due process of law.

Abused child—a child who has been physically, sexually, or mentally abused. Most states also consider a child abused who is forced into delinquent activity by a parent or guardian.

Acquittal—the judgment of a court, based on a verdict of a jury or a judicial officer, that the defendant is not guilty of the offense(s) for which he/she has been tried.

Actus reus—an act in violation of the law; a guilty act.

Adjudication—the process by which a court arrives at a decision regarding a case; also, the resultant decision.

Adjudicatory hearing—in juvenile justice usage, the fact-finding process wherein the juvenile court determines whether or not there is sufficient evidence to sustain the allegations in a petition.

ADMAX—administrative maximum; the term used by the federal government to denote ultra-high-security prisons.

Admission (Corrections)—in correctional usage, the entry of an offender into the legal jurisdiction of a corrections agency and/or physical custody of a correction facility.

Adult—in criminal justice usage, a person who is within the original jurisdiction of a criminal, rather than a juvenile, court because his or her age at the time of an alleged criminal act was above a statutorily specified limit.

Adversarial system—the two-sided structure under which American criminal courts operate and that pits the prosecution against the defense. In theory, justice is done when the most effective adversary is able to convince the judge or jury that their perspective on the case is the correct one.

Aftercare—in juvenile justice usage, the status or program

membership of a juvenile who has been committed to a treatment or confinement facility, conditionally released from the facility, and placed in a supervisory and/or treatment program.

Aggravated assault—unlawful intentional causing of serious bodily injury with or without a deadly weapon or unlawful intentional attempting or threatening of serious bodily injury or death with a deadly or dangerous weapon.

Aggravating circumstances—circumstances relating to the commission of a crime which cause its gravity to be greater than that of the average instance of the given type of offense.

Alias—any name used for an official purpose that is different from a person's legal name.

Alter ego rule—a rule of law that, in some jurisdictions, holds that a person can only defend a third party under circumstances and only to the degree that the third party could not act on their own behalf.

Alternative sanctions—See intermediate sanctions

Appeal—Generally, the request that a court with appellate jurisdiction review the judgment, decision, or order of a lower court and set it aside (reverse it) or modify it; also, the judicial proceedings or steps in judicial proceedings resulting from such a request.

Appearance (court)—the act of coming into a court and submitting to the authority of that court.

Appellant—the person who contests the correctness of a court order, judgment, or other decision and who seeks review and relief in a court having appellate jurisdiction, or the person in whose behalf this is done.

Appellate court—a court of which the primary function is to review the judgments of other courts and of administrative agencies.

Appellate jurisdiction—the lawful authority of a court to review a decision made by a lower court.

Arraignment—I. Strictly, the hearing before a court having jurisdiction in a criminal case, in which the identity of the defendant is established, the defendant is informed of the charge(s) and of his or her rights, and the defendant is required to enter a plea. II. In some usages, any appearance in court prior to trial in criminal proceedings.

Arrest— taking an adult or juvenile into physical custody by authority of law, for the purpose of charging the person with a criminal offense or a delinquent act or status offense, terminating with the recording of a specific offense.

Arrest (UCR)—In Uniform Crime Reports terminology, all separate instances where a person is taken into physical custody or notified or cited by a law enforcement officer or agency, except those relating to minor traffic violations.

Arrest rate—the number of arrests reported for each unit of population.

Arrest warrant—a document used by a judicial officer that directs a law enforcement officer to arrest an identified person who has been accused of a specific offense.

Arson—the intentional damaging or destruction, or attempted damaging or destruction, by means of fire or explosion of the property of another without the consent of the owner, or one's own property or that of another with intent to defraud.

Arson (UCR)—In Uniform Crime Reports terminology, the burning or attempted burning of property with or without intent to defraud.

Assault—unlawful intentional inflicting, or attempted or threatened inflicting, of injury upon the person of another.

Assault on a law enforcement officer—a simple or aggravated assault, where the victim is a law enforcement officer engaged in the performance of his/her duties.

Attendant circumstances—the facts surrounding an event.

Attorney—a person trained in the law, admitted to practice before the bar of a given jurisdiction, and authorized to advise, represent, and act for other persons in legal proceedings.

Backlog (court)—the number of cases awaiting disposition in a court which exceed the court's capacity for disposing of them within the period of time considered appropriate.

Bail—I. To effect the release of an accused person from custody, return for the promise that he or she will appear at a place and time specified and submit to the jurisdiction and judgment of the court, guaranteed by a pledge to pay to the court a specified sum of money or property if the person does not appear. II. The money or property pledged to the court or actually deposited with the court to effect the release of a person from legal custody.

Bail bond—a document guaranteeing the appearance of the defendant in court as required and recording the pledge of money or property to be paid to the court if he or she does not appear, which is signed by the person to be released and any other persons acting in his or her behalf.

Bail bondsman—a person, usually licensed, whose business it is to effect release on bail for persons charged with offenses and held in custody, by pledging to pay a sum of money if a defendant fails to appear in court as required.

Bailiff—the court officer whose duties are to keep order in the courtroom and to maintain physical custody of the jury.

Bail revocation—the court decision withdrawing that status of release on bail previously conferred upon a defendant.

Ballistics—the analysis of firearms, ammunition, projectiles, bombs, and explosions.

Battered woman's syndrome (BWS)—a series of common characteristics that appear on women who are abused physically and psychologically over an extended period of time by the dominant male figure in their lives; a pattern of psychological symptoms that develop after somebody has lived in a battering relationship; or a pattern of responses and perceptions presumed to be characteristic of women who have been subjected to continuous physical (and sexual) abuse by their mates.

Bench warrant—a document issued by a court directing that a law enforcement officer bring the person named therein before the court, usually one who has failed to obey a court order or a notice to appear.

Bind over—I. To require by judicial authority that a person promise to appear for trial, appear in court as a witness, or keep the peace. II. The decision by a court of limited jurisdiction requiring that a person charged with a felony appear for trial on that charge in a court of general jurisdiction, as the result of a finding of probable cause at a preliminary hearing held in the limited jurisdiction court.

Booking—a law enforcement or correctional administrative process officially recording an entry into detention after arrest, and identifying the person, the place, time, and reason for the arrest, and the arresting authority.

Broken window thesis—a perspective on crime causation which holds that physical deterioration in an area leads to increased concerns for personal safety among area residents, and to higher crime rates in that area.

Burglary—I. By the narrowest and oldest definition, trespassory breaking and entering of the dwelling house of another in the nighttime with the intent to commit a felony. II. Unlawful entry of any fixed structure, vehicle, or vessel used for regular residence, industry, or business, with or without force, with intent to commit a felony or larceny.

Capacity (legal)—in criminal justice usage, the legal ability of a person to commit a criminal act; the mental and physical ability to act with purpose and to be aware of the certain, probable, or possible results of one's conduct.

Capital offense—I. A criminal offense punishable by death. II. In some penal codes, an offense that may be punishable by death or by imprisonment for life.

Capital punishment—another term for the death penalty. Capital punishment is the most extreme of all sentencing options.

Career criminal—in prosecutorial and law enforcement usage, a person having a past record of multiple arrests or convictions for serious crimes, or an unusually large number of arrests or convictions for crimes of varying degrees.

Carnal knowledge—sexual intercourse, coitus, sexual copulation. Carnal knowledge is accomplished "if there is the slightest penetration of the sexual organ of the female by the sexual organ of the male."

Case law—that body of judicial precedent, historically built upon legal reasoning and past interpretations of statutory laws, which serves as a guide to decision making, especially in the courts.

Change of venue—the movement of a case from the jurisdiction of one court to that of another court that has the same subject matter jurisdictional authority but is in a different geographic location.

Charge—in criminal justice usage, an allegation that a specified person(s) has committed a specific offense, recorded in a functional document such as a record of arrest, a complaint, information or indictment, or a judgment of conviction.

Child abuse—the illegal physical, emotional, or sexual mistreatment of a child by his/her parent(s) or guardian(s).

Child neglect—the illegal failure by a parent(s) or guardian(s) to provide proper nourishment or care to a child.

Circumstantial evidence—evidence that requires interpretation or that requires a judge or jury to reach a conclusion based upon what the evidence indicates. From the close proximity of a smoking gun to the defendant, for example, the jury might conclude that he/she pulled the trigger.

Citation (to appear)—a written order issued by a law enforcement officer directing an alleged offender to appear in a specific court at a specific time in order to answer a criminal charge, and not permitting forfeit of bail as an alternative to court appearance.

Citizen's arrest—the taking of a person into physical custody, by a witness to a crime other than a law enforcement officer, for the purpose of delivering he or she to the physical custody of a law enforcement officer or agency.

Civil death—the legal status of prisoners in some jurisdictions who are denied the opportunity to vote, hold public office, marry, or enter into contracts by virtue of their status as incarcerated felons. While civil death is primarily of historical interest, some jurisdictions still place limits on the contractual opportunities available to inmates.

Civil law—that part of the law that governs relationship between parties.

Clearance (UCR)—the event where a known occurrence of a Part I offense is followed by an arrest or other decision which indicates a solved crime at the police level of reporting.

Clemency—in criminal justice usage, the name for the type of executive or legislative action where the severity of punishment of a single person or group of persons is reduced or the punishment stopped, or a person is exempted from prosecution for certain actions.

Closing argument—an oral summation of a case presented to a judge, or to a judge and jury, by the prosecution or by the defense in a criminal trial.

Commitment—the action of a judicial officer ordering that a person subject to judicial proceedings be placed in a particular kind of confinement or residential facility, for a specific reason authorized by law; also, the result of the action, the admission to the facility.

Common law—law originating from usage and custom rather than from written statutes. The term refers to a body of judicial opinion originally developed by English courts, and which is based upon non-statutory customs, traditions, and precedents.

Community service—a sentencing alternative that requires offenders to spend at least a part of their time working for a community agency.

Compelling interest—a legal concept that provides a basis for suspicionless searches (urinalysis tests of train engineers for example) when public safety is at issue.

Complaint—I. In general criminal justice usage, any accusation that a person(s) has committed an offense(s), received by or originating from a law enforcement or prosecutorial agency, or received by a court. II. In judicial process usage, a formal document submitted to the court by a prosecutor, law enforcement officer, or other person, alleging that a specified person(s) has committed a specified offense(s) and requesting prosecution.

Concurrence—the coexistence of an act in violation of the law, and a culpable mental state.

Concurrent sentence—a sentence that is one or two sentences imposed at the same time after conviction for more than one offense and to be served at the same time, or a new sentence imposed upon a person already under sentence(s) for a previous offense(s), to be served at the same time as one or more of the previous sentences.

Conditional release—the release by executive decision from a federal or state correctional facility, of a prisoner who has not served his or her full sentence and whose freedom is contingent upon obeying specified rules of behavior.

Conditions of probation and parole—the general (state-ordered) and special (court- or board-ordered) limits imposed upon an offender who is released on either probation or parole. General conditions tend to be fixed by state statute, while special conditions are mandated by the sentencing authority and take into consideration the background of the offender and circumstances surrounding the offense.

Confinement—in correctional terminology, physical restriction of a person to a clearly defined area from which he or she is lawfully forbidden to depart and from which departure is usually constrained by architectural barriers and/or guards or other custodians.

Consecutive sentence—a sentence that is one of two or more sentences imposed at the same time, after conviction for more than one offense, and which is served in sequence with the other sentences, or a new sentence for a new conviction, imposed upon a person already under sentence(s) for previous offense(s), which is added to a previous sentence(s), thus increasing the maximum time the offender may be confined or under supervision.

Contempt of court—intentionally obstructing a court in the administration of justice, or acting in a way calculated to lessen its authority or dignity, or failing to obey its lawful orders.

Conviction—the judgment of a court, based on the verdict of a jury or judicial officer, or on the guilty pleas or nolo contendere pleas of the defendant, that the defendant is guilty of the offense(s) with which he/she has been charged.

Correctional agency—a federal, state, or local criminal or juvenile agency, under a single administrative authority of which the principal functions are the intake screening, supervision, custody, confinement, treatment, or presentencing or predisposition investigation of alleged or adjudicated adult offenders, youthful offenders, delinquent, or status offenders.

Corrections—a generic term that includes all government agencies, facilities programs, procedures, personnel, and techniques concerned with the intake, custody, confinement, supervision, or treatment, or presentencing or predisposition investigation of alleged or adjudicated adult offenders, delinquents or status offenders.

Corruption—behavior deviation from an accepted ethical standard.

Corpus delicti—the "body of crime." Facts that show that a crime has occurred.

Court—an agency or unit of the judicial branch of government authorized or established by statute or constitution, and consisting of one or more judicial officers, which has the authority to decide upon cases, controversies in law, and disputed matters of fact brought before it.

Court clerk—an elected or appointed court officer responsible for maintaining the written records of the court and for supervising or performing the clerical tasks necessary for conducting judicial business; also, any employee of a court whose principal duties are to assist the court clerk in performing the clerical tasks necessary for conducting judicial business.

Court-martial—a military court convened by senior commanders under authority of the Uniform Code of Military Justice for the purpose of trying members of the armed forces accused of violations of the code.

Court of record—a court in which a complete and permanent record of all proceedings or specified types of proceedings is kept.

Court order—a mandate, command or direction issued by a judicial officer in the exercise of his or her judicial authority.

Court probation—a criminal court requirement that a defendant or offender fulfill specified conditions of behavior in lieu of a sentence to confinement, but without assignment to a probation agency's supervisory caseload.

Court reporter—a person present during judicial proceedings, who records all testimony and other oral statements made during the proceedings.

Crime—conduct in violation of the criminal laws of a state, the federal government, or a local jurisdiction, for which there is no legally acceptable justification or excuse. Also, an act committed or omitted in violation of a law forbidding or commanding it for which the possible penalties for an adult upon conviction include incarceration, for which a corporation can be penalized by fine or forfeit, or for which a juvenile can be adjudged delinquent or transferred to criminal court for prosecution.

Criminal homicide—the causing of the death of another person without legal justification or excuse.

Criminal law—that branch of modern law that concerns itself with offenses committed against society, members thereof, their property, and the social order.

Criminal negligence—behavior in which a person fails to reasonably perceive substantial and unjustifiable risks of dangerous consequences.

Criminal proceedings—the regular and orderly steps, as directed or authorized by statute or a court of law, taken to determine whether an adult accused of a crime is guilty or not guilty.

Criminalist—the term applied to police crime scene analysts and laboratory personnel versed in criminalistics.

Criminology—the scientific study of crime causation, prevention, and the rehabilitation and punishment of offenders.

Culpability—I. Blameworthiness; responsibility in some sense for an event or situation deserving of moral blame. II. In Model Penal Code (MPC) usage, a state of mind on the part of one who is committing an act, which makes him or her potentially subject to prosecution for that act.

Custody—legal or physical control of a person or thing; legal, supervisory, or physical responsibility for a person or thing.

Danger laws—those intended to prevent the pretrial release of criminal defendants judged to represent a danger to others in the community.

Dangerousness—the likelihood that a given individual will later harm society or others. Dangerousness is often measured in terms of recidivism, or as the likelihood of additional crime commission within a five-year period following arrest or release from confinement.

Deadly force—force likely to cause death or great bodily harm.

Deadly weapon—an instrument designed to inflict serious bodily injury or death, or capable of being used for such a purpose.

Defendant—in criminal justice usage, a person formally accused of an offense(s) by the filing in court of a charging document.

Defense counsel (attorney)—a licensed trial lawyer, hired or appointed to conduct the legal defense of an individual accused of a crime and to represent him or her before a court of law.

Defenses (to a criminal charge)—evidence and arguments offered by a defendant and his or her attorney(s) to show why that person should not be held liable for a criminal charge.

Delinquency—a juvenile who has been adjudged by a judicial officer of a juvenile court to have committed a delinquent act.

Deposition—a pretrial question-and-answer proceeding, usually conducted orally, in which a party or witness answers an attorney's questions. The answers are given under oath, and the session is recorded.

Detention—the legally authorized confinement of a person subject to criminal or juvenile court proceedings, until the point of commitment to a correctional facility or until release.

Diminished capability, also diminished responsibility—a defense based upon claims of a mental condition which may be insufficient to exonerate a defendant of guilt, but that may be relevant to specific mental elements of certain crimes or degrees of crimes.

Direct evidence—evidence that, if believed, directly proves a fact. Eyewitness testimony (and more recently, videotaped documentation) account for the majority of all direct evidence heard in the criminal courtroom.

Discharge—in criminal justice usage, to release from confinement or supervision or to release from a legal status imposing on obligation upon the subject person.

Disposition hearing—a hearing in juvenile court, conducted after an adjudicatory hearing and subsequent receipt of the report of any pre-disposition investigation, to determine the most appropriate form of custody and/or treatment for a juvenile who has been adjudged a delinquent, a status offender, or a dependent.

Diversion—the official suspension of criminal or juvenile proceedings against an alleged offender at any point after a recorded justice system intake but before the entering of a judgment and referral of that person to a treatment or care program administered by a nonjustice agency, or no referral.

DNA profiling—the use of biological residue found at the scene of a crime for genetic comparisons in aiding the identification of criminal suspects.

Double jeopardy—a common law and constitutional prohibition against a second trial for the same offense.

Drug abuse—illicit drug use that results in social, economic, psychological, or legal problems for the user.

Due process of law—a right guaranteed by the Fifth, Sixth, and Fourteenth Amendments of the US Constitution, and generally understood, in legal contexts, to mean the due course of legal proceedings according to the rules and forms which have been established for the protection of private rights.

Element of a crime—I. any conduct, circumstance, or state of mind which in combination with other conduct, circumstance, or states of mind constitute an unlawful act; II. the basic components of crime; (III) in a specific crime, the essential features of that crime as specified by law or statute.

Emergency searches—those searches conducted by the police without a warrant, that are justified on the basis of some immediate and overriding need, such as public safety, the likely escape of a dangerous suspect, or the removal or destruction of evidence.

Entrapment—an improper or illegal inducement to crime by agents of enforcement. Also, a defense that may be raised when such inducements occur.

Evidence—anything useful to a judge or jury in deciding the facts of a case. Evidence may take the form of witness testimony, written documents, videotapes, magnetic media, photographs, physical objects, etc.

Exclusionary rule—the understanding, based on Supreme Court precedent, that incriminating information must be seized according to constitutional specifications of due process, or it will not be allowed as evidence in criminal trials.

Excuses—a category of legal defenses in which the defendant claims that some personal condition or circumstance at the time of the act was such that he or she should not be held accountable under the criminal law.

Expert witness—a person who has special knowledge recognized by the court as relevant to the determination of guilt or innocence. Expert witnesses may express opinions or draw conclusions in their testimony, unlike lay witnesses.

Extradition—the surrender by one state to another of an individual accused or convicted of an offense in the second state.

Felony—a criminal offense punishable by death or by incarceration in a prison facility.

Filing—the initiation of a criminal case in a court by formal submission to the court of a charging document, alleging that one or more named persons have committed one or more specified criminal offenses.

Fine—the penalty imposed upon a convicted person by a court, requiring that he or she pay a specific sum of money to the court.

First appearance (initial appearance)—an appearance before a magistrate which entails the process whereby the legality of a defendant's arrest is initially assessed, and he or she is informed of the charges on which he/she is being held. At this stage in the criminal justice process bail may be set or pretrial release arranged.

Good time—in correctional usage, the amount of time deducted from time to be served in prison on a given sentence(s) and/or under correctional agency jurisdiction, at some point after a prisoner's admission to prison, contingent upon good behavior and/or awarded automatically by application of a statute or regulation.

Grand jury—a body of persons who have been selected according to law and sworn to hear the evidence against accused persons and determine whether there is sufficient evidence to bring those persons to trial, to investigate criminal activity generally, and to investigate the conduct of public agencies and officials.

Guilty but mentally ill—equivalent to finding a "guilty," a GMMI verdict establishes that the defendant, although mentally ill, was in sufficient possession of his faculties to be morally blameworthy for his acts.

Guilty plea—a defendant's formal answer in court to the charge(s) contained in a complaint, information, or indictment that he or she did commit the offense(s) listed.

Habeas corpus—a writ requiring a person to be brought before a judge or into court, especially to investigate the lawfulness of his or her detention.

Hate crimes—criminal offense in which the defendant's conduct was motivated by hatred, bias, or prejudice, based on the actual or perceived race, color, religion. National origin, ethnicity, gender, or sexual orientation of another individual or group of individuals.

Hearing—a proceeding in which arguments, witnesses, or evidence are heard by a judicial officer or administrative body.

Hearsay rule—the long-standing American courtroom precedent that hearsay cannot be used in court. Rather than accepting testimony based upon hearsay, the American trial process asks that the person who was the original source of the hearsay information be brought into court to be questioned and cross-examined. Exceptions to the hearsay rule may occur when the person with direct knowledge is dead or is otherwise unable to testify.

Hung jury—a jury that after long debate is so irreconcilably divided in opinion that it is unable to reach any verdict.

Hypothesis—I. An explanation that accounts for a set of facts and that can be tested by further investigation. II. Something that is taken to be true for the purpose of argument or investigation.

Illegal search and seizure—an act in violation of the Fourth Amendment of the US Constitution: "The right of people to be secure in their persons, houses, papers, and effects, against unreasonable searches and seizures, shall not be violated, and no warrants shall issue but upon probable cause, supported by oath or affirmation, and particularly describing the place to be searched and the persons or things to be seized."

Illegally seized evidence—evidence seized in opposition to the principles of due process was described by the Bill of Rights. Most illegally seized evidence is the result of police searches conducted without a proper warrant, or improperly conducted interrogations.

Inchoate offense—one not yet completed. Also, an offense that consists of an action or conduct that is a step toward the intended commission of another offense.

Included offense—an offense that is made up of elements that are a subset of the elements or another offense having a greater statutory penalty, and the occurrence of which is established by the same evidence or by some portion of the evidence that has been offered to establish the occurrence of the greater offense.

Incompetent to stand trial—in criminal proceedings, the finding by a court that a defendant is mentally incapable of understanding the nature of the charges and proceedings against him or her, of consulting with an attorney, and of aiding in his or her own defense.

Indeterminate sentence—a type of sentence to imprisonment where the commitment, instead of being for a specified single time quantity, such as three years, is for a range of time, such as two to five years or five years maximum and zero minimum.

Indictment—a formal, written accusation submitted to the court by a grand jury, alleging that a specific person(s) has committed a specific offense(s), usually a felony.

Individual rights—those guaranteed to all members of our society by the US Constitution. These rights are especially relevant to criminal defendants facing formal professing by the criminal justice system.

Initial plea (first plea)—the first plea to a given charge entered in the court record by or for the defendant. The acceptance of an initial plea by the court unambiguously indicated that the arraignment process has been completed.

Insanity defense—a defense that claims that the person charged with a crime did not know what they were doing, or that they did not know what they were doing was wrong.

Intensive probation—a form of probation supervision involving frequent face-to-face contacts between the probationary client and probation officers.

Intent—the state of mind or attitude with which an act is carried out; the design, resolve, or determination with which a person acts to achieve a certain result.

Intermediate sanctions (alternative sanctions)—the use of split sentencing, shock probation and parole, home confinement, shock incarceration, and community service in lieu of other, more traditional, sanctions such as imprisonment and fines. Intermediate sanctions are becoming increasingly popular as prison crowding grows.

Interrogation—the information gathering activities of police officers that involve the direct questioning of suspects.

Judgment—the court's final decision regarding the rights and claims of the parties to a lawsuit.

Jurisprudence—the philosophy of law; the science and study of law.

Juror—a member of a trial or grand jury, selected for jury duty, and required to serve as an arbiter of the facts in a court of law.

Jury panel—the group of persons summoned to appear in court as potential jurors for a particular trial, or the persons selected from the group of potential jurors to sit in the jury box, from which second group those acceptable to the prosecution and the defense are finally chosen as the jury.

Just deserts—as a model of criminal sentencing, one that holds that criminal offenders deserve the punishment they receive at the hands of the law, and that punishments should be appropriate to the type and severity of the crime committed.

Justifications—a category of legal defenses in which the defendant admits committing the act in question, but claims it was necessary in order to avoid some greater evil.

Kidnapping—transpiration or confinement of a person without authority of law and without his or her consent, or without the consent of his or her guardian, if a minor.

Lay witness—an eyewitness, character witness, or any other person called upon to testify who is not considered an expert. Lay witnesses must testify to facts alone and may not draw conclusions or express opinions.

Legal cause—a legally recognizable cause. The type of cause is required to be demonstrated in court in order to hold an individual criminally liable for causing harm.

Lex talionis—the law of retaliation, often expressed as "an eye for an eye," or like for like.

M. Naghten Rule—a rule for determining insanity that asks whether the defendant knew what he was doing, or whether he knew that what he was doing was wrong.

Mala in se—acts that are regarded as wrong in themselves.

Mala prohibita—acts that are considered "wrongs" only because there is a law against them.

Mandatory sentence—a statutory requirement that a certain penalty shall be set and carried out in all cases upon conviction for a specified offense or series of offenses.

Maximum sentence—I. In legal usage, the maximum penalty provided by law for a given criminal offense, usually stated as maximum term of imprisonment or a maximum fine. II. In correctional usage in relation to a given offender, any of several quantities which vary according to whether calculated at the point of sentencing or at a later point in the correctional process, and according to whether the time period referred to as the term of confinement or the total period under correctional jurisdiction.

Mens rea—the state of mind that accompanies a criminal act. Also, guilty mind.

Miranda Rights—the set of rights that a person accused or suspected of having committed a specific offense has during interrogation, and of which he or she must be informed prior to questioning, as stated by the U.S. Supreme Court.

Misdemeanor—on offense punishable by incarceration, usually in a local confinement facility, for a period of which the upper limit is prescribed by statute in a given jurisdiction, typically limited to a year or less.

Mistrial—a trial that has been terminated or declared invalid by the court because of some circumstance that creates a substantial and uncorrectable prejudice to the conduct of a fair trial. Or which makes it impossible to continue the trial in accordance with prescribed procedures.

Mitigating circumstances—circumstances surrounding the commission of a crime which do not in law justify or excuse the act, but which in fairness may be considered as reducing the blameworthiness of the defendant.

Motion—an oral or written request made to a court at any time before, during, or after court proceedings, asking the court to make a specific finding, decision, or order.

Motive—a person's reason for committing a crime.

Murder and nonnegligent manslaughter—intentionally causing the death of another without legal justification or excuse, or causing the death of another while committing or attempting to commit another crime.

Neglected child—a child who is not receiving the proper level of physical or psychological care from his or her parents or guardian, or who has been placed up for adoption in violation of the law.

Negligence—in legal usage, generally, a state of mind accompanying a person's conduct such that he or she is not aware, though a reasonable person should be aware, that there is a risk that the conduct might cause a particular harmful result.

Negligent manslaughter—causing death of another by recklessness or gross negligence.

Nolle prosequi—a formal entry upon the record of the court, indicating that the prosecutor declares that he or she will proceed no further in the action. The terminating of adjudication of a criminal charge by the prosecutor's decision not to pursue the case, in some jurisdictions requires the approval of the court.

Nolo contendere—a plea of "no contest." A no contest plea may be used where the defendant does not wish to contest conviction. Because the plea does not admit guilt, however, it cannot provide the basis for later civil suits that might follow upon the heels of a criminal conviction.

Not guilty by reason of insanity—the plea of a defendant or the verdict of a jury in a criminal proceeding, that the defendant is not guilty of the offense(s) charged because at the time the crime(s) was committed the defendant did not have the mental capacity to be held criminally responsible for his or her actions.

No true bill—the decision by a grand jury that it will not return an indictment against the person(s) accused of a crime(s) on the basis of the allegations and evidence presented by the prosecutor.

Offender—an adult who has been convicted of a criminal offense.

Offense—I. a violation of the criminal law, or in some jurisdictions II. a minor crime sometimes described as "ticketable."

Opening statement—the initial statement of an attorney (or of a defendant representing himself or herself) made in a court of law to a judge or to a judge and jury, describing the facts that he or she intends to present during trial in order to prove his or her case.

Opinion—the official announcement of a decision of a court together with the reasons for that decision.

Parole—the status of an offender conditionally released from a prison by discretion of a paroling authority prior to expiration of sentence, requires observing conditions of parole, and placed under the supervision of a parole agency.

Parole board—a state paroling authority. Most states have parole boards that decide when an incarcerated offender is ready for conditional release and that may also function as revocation hearing panels.

Parole revocation—the administrative action of a paroling authority removing a person from parole status in response to a violation of lawfully required condition of parole including the prohibition against commissions of a new offense, and usually resulting in a return to prison.

Peremptory challenge—the right to challenge a juror without assigning a reason for the challenge. In most jurisdictions each party to an action, both civil and criminal, has specified number of such challenges and after using all preemptory challenges, have to furnish a reason for subsequent challenges.

Perjury—the intentional making of a false statement as part of testimony by a sworn witness in a judicial proceeding on a matter material to the inquiry.

Perpetrator—the chief actor in the commission of a crime, that is, the person who directly commits the criminal act.

Petition—a written request made to a court asking for the exercise of its judicial powers or asking for permission to perform some act where the authorization of a court is required.

Plaintiff—a person who initiates a court action.

Plea—in criminal proceedings, a defendant's formal answer in court to the charge contained in a complaint, information, or indictment, that he or she is guilty or not guilty of the offense charges, or does not contest the charge.

Plea bargaining—the negotiated agreement between defendant, prosecutor, and the court as to what an appropriate plea and associated sentence should be in a given case. Plea-bargaining circumvents the trial process and dramatically reduces the time required for the resolution of a criminal case. It generally involves the defendants pleading guilty to a lesser offense in return for a lighter sentence.

Postconviction remedy—the procedure or set of procedures by which a person who has been convicted of a crime can challenge in court the lawfulness of a judgment of conviction or penalty or of a correctional agency action, and thus obtain relief in situations where this cannot be done by a direct appeal.

Precedent—a legal principal that operated to ensure that previous judicial decision are authoritatively considered and incorporated into future cases.

Preliminary hearing—the proceeding before a judicial officer in which three matters must be decided—whether a crime was committed, whether the crime occurred within the territorial jurisdiction of the court, and whether there are reasonable grounds to believe that the defendant committed the crime.

Presentence investigation—the examination of a convicted offender's background prior to sentencing. Presentence examinations are generally conducted by probation/parole officers and submitted to sentencing authorities.

Pretrial detention—any period of confinement occurring between arrest and other holding to answer a charge and the conclusion of prosecution.

Pretrial discovery—in criminal proceedings, disclosure by the prosecution or the defense prior to trail of evidence or other information which is intended to be used in the trial.

Pretrial release—the release of an accused from custody. For all or part of the time before or during prosecution, upon his or her promise to appear in court when required.

Probable cause—a set of facts and circumstances that would induce a reasonably intelligent and prudent person to believe that a particular person had committed a specific crime; reasonable grounds to make or believe an accusation. Probable cause is needed for a "full blown" search or arrest.

Probation—a sentence of imprisonment that is suspended. Also, the conditional freedom granted by a judicial officer to an adjudicated adult or juvenile offender, as long as the person meets certain conditions of behavior.

Procedural defense—a defense that claims that the defendant was in some significant way discriminated against in the judicial process or that some important aspect of official procedure was not properly followed in the investigation or prosecution of the crime charged.

Proportionality—a sentencing principle that holds that the severity of the sanctions should bear a direct relationship to the seriousness of the crime committed.

Prosecutor—an attorney who is elected or appointed chief of a prosecution agency, and whose official duty is to conduct criminal proceedings on behalf of the people against persons accused of committing criminal offenses. Also called "district attorney," "DA," "state's attorney," "county attorney," and "U.S. attorney" and any attorney deputized to assist the chief prosecutor.

Psychopath or sociopath—a person with a personality disorder, especially one manifested in aggressively antisocial behavior, which is often said to be the result of a poorly developed superego.

Psychosis—a form of mental illness in which sufferers are said to be out of touch with reality.

Public defender—an attorney employed by a government agency or subagency, or by a private organization under contract to a unit of government, for the purpose of providing defense services to indigents; also occasionally, an attorney who has volunteered such service. The head of a government agency or subunit whose function is the representation in court of persons accused or convicted of a crime who are unable to hire private counsel, and any attorney employed by such an agency or subunit whose official duty is the performance of the indigent defense function.

Punitive damages—damages that are awarded in a civil lawsuit to punish the wrongdoer. Punitive damages are usually awarded only in cases involving willful or malicious misconduct.

Rape—unlawful sexual intercourse, achieved through force and without consent. May include same sex rape.

Reasonable doubt—an actual and substantial doubt arising from the evidence, from the facts or circumstances shown by the evidence, or from the lack of evidence. Also, that state of the case that, after the entire comparison and consideration of all the evidence, leaves the minds of the jurors in that condition that they cannot say that they feel an abiding conviction of the truth of the charge.

Reasonable doubt standard—that standard of proof necessary for conviction in criminal trials.

Recidivism—the repetition of criminal behavior.

Release on recognizance—the pretrial release of a criminal defendant on their written promise to return to appear. No cash or property bond is required.

Reprieve—an executive act temporarily suspending the execution of a sentence, usually a death sentence. A reprieve differs from other suspensions of sentence not only in that it almost always applies to temporary withdrawing of a death sentence, but also in that it usually is an act of clemency intended to provide the prisoner with time to secure amelioration of the sentence.

Reasonable suspicion—I. That level of suspicion that would justify an officer in making further inquiry or in conducting further investigation. Reasonable suspicion may permit a simple "stop and frisk." II. A belief based upon a consideration of the facts at hand and upon reasonable inferences drawn from those facts, which would induce an ordinarily prudent and cautious person under the same circumstance to generally conclude that criminal activity is taking place or that criminal activity has recently occurred.

Restitution—a court requirement that an alleged or convicted offender pays money or provides services to the victim of the crime or provides services to the community.

Retribution—the act of taking revenge upon a criminal perpetrator.

Rules of evidence—rules of court that govern the admissibility of evidence at a criminal hearing and trial.

Sentence—the penalty imposed by a court upon a person convicted of a crime.

Sentencing dispositions—court dispositions of defendants after judgment of conviction, expressed as penalties, such as imprisonment or payment of fines; or any number of alternatives to actually executed penalties, such as suspended sentences, grants of probation, court orders to perform restitution; or various combinations of the foregoing.

Sentencing hearing—in criminal proceedings, a hearing during which the court or jury considers relevant information, such as evidence concerning aggravating or mitigating circumstances, for the purpose of determining a sentencing disposition for a person convicted of an offense(s).

Sequestered jury—a jury that is isolated from the public during the course of the trial and throughout the deliberation process.

Shock incarceration—a sentencing option that makes use of "boot camp"-type prisons in order to impress upon convicted offenders the realities of prison life.

Speedy trial—a trial that is held in a timely manner. The right of a defendant to have a prompt trial is guaranteed by the Sixth Amendment of the US Constitution.

Split sentence—a sentence explicitly requiring the convicted person to serve a period of confinement in a local, state, or federal facility followed by a period of probation.

Stare decisis—the legal principle that requires that courts be bound by their own earlier decisions and by those of higher courts having jurisdiction over them regarding subsequent cases on similar issues of law and fact. The term literally means "standing by decided matters."

Statutory law—written or codified law. The law on the books, enacted by a governmental body or agency having power to make laws.

Stay of execution—the stopping by a court of the carrying out or implementation of a judgment, that is, of a court order previously issued.

Subpoena—a document commanding a person to appear at a certain time and place to give testimony concerning a certain matter.

Supervised probation—guidance, treatment, or regulation by a probation agency of the behavior of the person who is subject to adjudication or who had been convicted of an offense, resulting from a formal court order or a probation agency decision.

Suspect—an adult or juvenile considered by a criminal justice agency to be one who may have committed a specific criminal offense, but who has not been arrested or charged.

Suspended sentence—the court decision to delay imposing or executing a penalty for a specified or unspecified period, also called "sentence withheld." A court disposition of a convicted person pronouncing a penalty of a fine or commitment to confinement, but unconditionally discharging the defendant or holding execution of the penalty in abeyance upon good behavior.

Testimony—oral evidence offered by a sworn witness on the witness stand during a criminal trial.

Total institutions—enclosed facilities, separated from society both socially and physically, where the inhabitants share all aspects of their lives on a daily basis.

Trial—the examination in a court of the issues of fact and law in a case, for the purpose of reaching a judgment. In criminal proceedings, the examination in a court of the issues of fact and law in a case, for the purpose of reaching a judgment of conviction or acquittal of the defendant(s).

Trial de novo—literally, a new trial. The term is applied to cases that are retried on appeal, as opposed to those that are simply reviewed on the record.

Truth in sentencing—a close correspondence between the sentence imposed upon those sent to prison and the time actually served prior to prison release.

Unconditional release—the final release of an offender from the jurisdiction of a correctional agency; a final release from the jurisdiction of a court.

Verdict—in criminal proceedings, the decision of the jury in a jury trial or of a judicial officer in a non-jury trial.

Victim—a person who has suffered death, physical or mental anguish, or loss of property as the result of an actual or attempted criminal offense committed by another person.

Victim assistance program—an organized program which offers services to victims of crime in the areas of crisis intervention and follow-up counseling, and which helps victims secure their rights under the law.

Victim impact statement—the in-court use of victim- or survivor-supplied information by sentencing authorities wishing to make an informed sentencing decision.

Violent crime—murder, rape, aggravated assault, and robbery.

Warrant—any of a number of writs issued by a judicial officer, which direct a law enforcement officer to perform a specified act and afford him protection from damage if he performs it.

Weapons offense—unlawful sale, distribution, manufacture, alteration, transportation, possession, or use or attempted sale, distribution, manufacture, alteration, transportation, possession, or use of a deadly or dangerous weapon or accessory.

Witness—a person who is asked to testify under oath at a trial.

Writ—a document issued by a judicial officer ordering or forbidding the performance of a specified act.

Writ of habeas corpus—the writ that directs the person detaining a prisoner to bring him/her before a judicial officer to determine the lawfulness of the imprisonment.

Bibliography of Additional Readings

Allen, N. H. (1991). Survivor victims of homicide: Murder is only the beginning. In D. Leviton (Ed.), *Horrendous death and health: Toward action* (pp. 5-23). New York: Hemisphere.

Bard, M., Arnone, H. C., & Nemiroff, D. (1986). Contextual influences on the posttraumatic stress adaptation of homicide survivor victims. In C. Figley (Ed.), *Trauma and its wake: U.S. traumatic stress theory, research, and intervention* (Vol. 2) (pp. 292-304). New York: Brunner/Mazel.

Barkas, J. L. (1978). *Victims.* New York: Charles Scriber's Sons.

Brehony, K. A. (2000). *After the darkest hour: How suffering begins the journey to wisdom.* New York: Henry Holt.

Brothers, J. (1990). *Widowed.* New York: Simon & Schuster.

Burman, S., & Allen-Meares, P. (1994). Neglected victims of murder: Children's witness to parental homicide. *Social Work, 39*(1), 28-34.

Colgrove, M., Bloomfield, H., & McWilliams, P. (1991). *How to survive the loss of a love.* Los Angeles, CA: Prelude Press.

Counts, D. R., & Counts, D. A. (1991). *Coping with the final tragedy: Cultural variation in dying and grieving.* Amityville, NY: Baywood.

Doka, K. (Ed.). (1996). *Living with grief after sudden loss*. Bristol, PA: Taylor & Francis.

Dyson, J. L. (1990). The effect of family violence on children's academic performance and behavior. *Journal of the National Medical Association*, 82(1), 17-22.

Felber, M. (1997). *Grief expressed when a mate dies*. West Fork, AR: Lifeworlds.

Figley, C. R. (1985). From victim to survivor: Social responsibility in the wake of catastrophe. In Figley, C.R. (Ed). *Trauma and its wake: The study and treatment of posttraumatic stress disorder* (pp. 398-415). New York: Brunner/Mazel.

Figley, C. (1986). *Trauma and its wake*. New York: Brunner/Mazel.

Figley, C. R. (1995). Systemic PTSD: Family treatment experiences and implications. In G. S. Everly, J. M. Latting, et al. (Eds.) *Psychotraumatology: Key papers and core concepts in posttraumatic stress* (pp. 341-358). New York: Plenum Press.

Frieze, I. H., Hymer, S., & Greenberg, M. S. (1987). Describing the crime victim: Psychological reactions to victimization. *Professional Psychological Research Practice,* 18(4), 299-315.

Gauthier, J., & Marshall, W. L. (1977). Grief: A cognitive-behavioral analysis. *Cognitive Therapy Research*, 1, 34-44.

Gayton, P. R. (1995). *The forgiving place: Choosing peace after violent trauma*. Waco, TX: WRS Publishing.

Getzel, G. S., & Masters, R. (1984). Serving families who survive homicide. *Social Casework*, 4, 138-144.

Holstein, J. A., & Gubrium, J. F. (1995). *The active interview*. Thousand Oaks, CA: Sage.

Horowitz, M. J., Wilner, N., Kaltreider, N., & Alvarez, W. (1980). Signs and symptoms of posttraumatic tress disorder. *Archives of General Psychiatry*, 37, 85-92.

Lazarus, R. S. (1985). The psychology of stress and coping. *Mental Health Nursing*, 7, 1-4, 399-418.

Lyon, E., Moore, N., & Lexius, C. (1992). Group work with families of homicide victims. *Social Work into Groups*, 15, 19-33.

MacLaren, W. H. (1980). The deceased other: Presence and absence. *Dissertation Abstracts*, 41(6-B), 2332.

McCracken, A., & Semel, M. (Eds.). (1998). *A broken heart still beats: When your child dies*. Center City, MN: Hazelden.

Morris, C. W. (Ed.). (1934). *The works of George Herbert Mead: Mind, self, society*. Chicago: The University of Chicago Press.

National Organization for Victim Assistance. (1985, October). Survivors of homicide victims. *Network Information Bulletin*, 2(3), 1-10.

Peterson, C., & Seligman, M. (1983). Learned helplessness and victimization. *Journal of Social Issues*, 39, 113-116.

Ramsay, R. (1977). Behavioural approaches to bereavement. *Behaviour Research & Therapy*, 15(2), 131-135.

Rando, T. A. (1988). *How to go on living when someone you love dies*. Lexington, MA: Lexington Books.

Range, L. M., & Niss, N. M. (1990). Long-term bereavement from suicide, homicide, accidents and natural death. *Death Studies*, 14, 423-433.

Rinear, E. E. (1985, April 22). *Signs and symptoms of posttraumatic stress disorder among surviving parents of child homicide victims*. Paper presented at the 62nd Annual Meeting of the American Orthopsychiatric Association, New York.

Schutz, A. (1970). *On phenomenology and social relations*. Chicago: The University of Chicago Press.

Silverman, P. R. (1981). *Helping women cope with grief*. Newbury Park: Sage.

Smith, M. D., & Zahn, N. A. (Eds.). (1999). *Studying and preventing homicide*. Thousand Oaks, CA: Sage.

Smith, M., & Zahn, N. A. (Eds.). (1999). *Homicide a sourcebook of social research*. Thousand Oaks, CA: Sage.

Wolfelt, A. D. (1992). *Understanding grief helping yourself heal*. Bristol, PA: Accelerated Development.

Index

How to Write
Comforting Letters to the Bereaved:
A Simple Guide for a Delicate Task

John D. Haley

The Magical Thoughts of Grieving Children:
Treating Children with Complicated Mourning
and Advice for Parents

James A. Fogarty

Grieving Reproduction Loss:
The Healing Process

Kathleen Gray and Anne Lassance

Living Victims, Stolen Lives:
Parents of Murdered Children
Speak to America

Brad Stetson

Prospects for Immortality:
A Sensible Search for Life After Death

J. Robert Adams

Death and Bereavement
around the World, Volume 1:
Major Religious Traditions

edited by John D. Morgan and Pittu Laungani

Making Sense of Death:
Spiritual, Pastoral, and Personal Aspects of Death,
Dying and Bereavement

edited by Gerry R. Cox,
Robert A. Bendiksen, and Robert G. Stevenson